The Movement of Thought

The Movement of Thought

An Essay on Intellect in Seventeenth-Century France

Herbert De Ley

UNIVERSITY OF ILLINOIS PRESS

Urbana and Chicago

Publication of this work was supported in part
by a grant from the Campus Research Board,
University of Illinois — Urbana-Champaign.

This book is printed on acid-free paper.

Library of Congress Cataloging in Publication Data

De Ley, Herbert.
  The movement of thought.

  Bibliography: p.
  Includes index.
  1. French literature—17th century—History and
criticism.   2. Philosophy in literature.   3. France—
Intellectual life—17th century.   I. Title.
PQ245.D4   1985   840′.9′004   84-16128
ISBN 0-252-01165-1 (alk. paper)

CONTENTS

PREFACE

CONTINUOUS INTEREST over the last three or four decades has made seventeenth-century France a kind of model case of stylistic and intellectual change. In recent years studies of the subject have seemed on the verge of major advances; however, the question of just what movement may actually have taken place—and indeed the methodological problem of how intellectual movement may best be understood and described—continues to present serious difficulties. The purpose of this book is to contribute to understanding of the movement of intellect in France—and to a lesser extent in Europe—in the seventeenth century.

Anyone attempting to discuss a topic so extensively studied must necessarily touch on the work of many researchers. The problem is complicated, moreover, by the well-known methodological divisions between literary historians, new critics, structuralists, semioticians, Foucaldians, and the like. Interesting studies continue to appear (an example might be Jeanne Haight's instructive *The Concept of Reason in French Classical Literature, 1635–1690* [Toronto: University of Toronto Press, 1982]) more or less without reference to recent critical constructs. Other studies (Michel Foucault and the semioticians, for example) have presented themselves as so revolutionary as to render superfluous references to critics before 1970 or 1960.

The present study applies a considerable variety of methods to a small number of texts. Phenomenologically, or skeptically, or empirically inclined, I have been more impressed by the complementarity and mutual reinforcement of varying methods than by the exclusive claims of any one of them. As a phenomenologically inclined writer, I do not share some literary historians' distaste for structuralist or semiotic approaches. Nor do I share some semioticians' impatience with preceding schools. Instead, I find any one of a variety of views illuminating, some perhaps more than others in specific contexts, and a variety better than any one—and thus seek eclectic or syncretistic insight in a field currently marked by doctrinal controversies. Anyone attempting such a feat risks falling, as the French say, between a great many horses; he may also hope, however, to discover a convergence, a kind of *fond* of statement held in common among various commentators. The result may contribute something to the critique of methodologies, but will contribute more to understanding of the subject itself.

In any case I wish to acknowledge considerable debts to a variety of teachers—to Antoine Adam, Imbrie Buffum, Henri Peyre, and, most particularly, Judd D. Hubert—to all of whom I express sincere and deep admiration and gratitude. I also thank others mentioned more specifically in the following pages—which references, however, cannot pretend to do justice to the extensive related commentary. A portion of this book has appeared in the *Yale French Studies* in an issue devoted to "Science, Literature, and the Perceptive Mind" (no. 49 [1973]; T. J. Reiss, editor) and is reproduced here, in part, with the editor's permission. A related article, "Deux Erotismes, deux modes de pensée dans les *Galanteries du duc d'Ossonne*," appeared in *La Cohérence intérieure* (Paris: J.-M. Place, 1977). Papers peripheral to it have been read in the Modern Language Association of America's Literature and Science Division ("The Elizabethan World Picture Revisited"—1976) and Seventeenth-Century Literature Section ("The Non-Reader in Seventeenth-Century France"—1976; rpt., *PFSCL* 6 [1976–77]), and the French Literature Conference ("'Dans les reigles du plaisir': Transformations of Sexual Knowledge in Seventeenth-Century France"—1982; rpt. Leiner, etc.).

Thanks are due to the staff of the British Museum and the Bibliothèque Nationale, as well as to the Research Board and Library and library staff of the University of Illinois, and to the College of Letters and Science of the University of California at Los Angeles for their support. A number of persons, finally, have helped to bring this work to its present state. They include my wife, Margo Ynes Corona De Ley, and research assistants Madame Danielle Hilson, Madame Jacqueline Van Landeghem Parker, and Mss. Dianne Andrews, Judy Checker, Elizabeth Downs, Jane Merino Morais, and Judy Sherman, who gave indispensable help in assembling material for the project. Professors George Francis, Peter Haidu, Judd D. Hubert, and Robert J. Nelson read the manuscript or parts of it and offered helpful suggestions.

L'empirisme n'est nullement une réaction contre les concepts, ni un simple appel à l'expérience vécue. Il entreprend au contraire la plus folle création. . . . L'empirisme, c'est le mysticisme du concept, et son mathématisme. Mais précisément il traite le concept comme l'objet d'une rencontre, comme un ici-maintenant, ou plutôt comme un *Erewhon* d'où sortent, inépuisables, les "ici" et les "maintenant" toujours nouveaux, autrement distribués. . . . Je fais, refais et défais mes concepts à partir d'un horizon mouvant . . .

[Empiricism is not at all a reaction against concepts, nor a simple appeal to experience. On the contrary, it undertakes a most insane creation. . . . Empiricism is the mysticism of the concept, and its mathematization. Indeed, it treats concepts as the object of an encounter, as a here-and-now, or rather, as an *Erewhon* from which come inexhaustibly new "heres" and new "nows," differently distributed. . . . I make, remake, and unmake my concepts to match a moving horizon . . .].

—Gilles Deleuze, *Différence et répétition*

CHAPTER 1

Some Models of Intellectual Movement

FOR SOME READERS the very notion of intellectual movement is a false problem. A persistent view holds that literature and philosophy are a kind of repetition of eternal values or—as many in the seventeenth century believed as well—a continuing conversation with the great minds of the past. Others imply that any possible movement of thought is purely a matter of personalities, groups, discoveries, influences, and reactions. Yet even those inclined to see nothing more than event following event are occasionally led to speak of tendencies somehow independent of individuals.

The intellectual "archeologist" Michel Foucault speaks of "les familiarités de la pensée" ["the familiar territories of thought"] and wonders how, in some given intellectual context, certain thoughts might be impossible to think: "Qu'est-il donc impossible de penser, et de quelle impossibilité s'agit-il?" ["What may thus be impossible to think, and what sort of impossibility is it?"]. Working in a very different tradition, Henri Peyre writes skeptically that "everything always coexisted" and considers "the assumption that a certain view of the world and a certain philosophy inform all the manifestations of a given age" to be "gratuitous." He also muses, however, on the apparent mystery of obvious time-specific differences in discourse: "Why do most of the great talents of a certain era seem to align themselves behind a few common trends, as the classical writers of France did in 1660–85, [or] the *philosophes* a century later when no writer, among the thousands who attempted it, succeeded in defending religion with any brilliance. . . ." And even the conservative literary historian Antoine Adam writes, as he describes certain reforms associated with the early seventeenth-century poet Malherbe, that "Cette tendance, nous l'avons observée, à l'aube même du siècle. . . . Elle est donc antérieure à l'arrivée de Malherbe à Paris. Elle existe indépendamment de lui. Elle se développe près de lui dans des cercles qui lui restent pourtant étrangers, comme celui de Piat Maucors. Elle persiste après lui, au point que Des Marests, en 1633, croira nécessaire de protester contre ses excès. En fait, tous les écrivains ont été plus ou moins marqués par elle" ["We have observed this tendency even at the very beginning of the century. . . . It thus predates Malherbe's arrival in Paris. It exists independently of him. It develops around him in circles of which he was ignorant, like that of Piat Maucors. It persists after him, so much so that Des Marests, in 1633, will believe it necessary to protest against its excesses. In fact, every writer was more or less touched by it"].[1]

As soon as the notion of "impossibility" or "trend" or "tendency" is introduced, however, the problem of intellectual change acquires an additional dimension—one or another concept of metaorder or metacausality, operating somehow "behind" or "beneath" simple events. Thinking along these lines, some writers have celebrated the overriding influence of certain towering intellectual giants—like Descartes or Newton or Voltaire. Others have celebrated great ages—an Elizabethan Age or a Golden Age or a *Grand Siècle* or a Century of Louis XIV. Yet other writers describe a Mannerist Period, or a Baroque Period, informing not only painting, sculpture, and architecture, but also literature and other intellectual disciplines as well.

Over the last few decades, studies of mannerist and baroque intellectual styles have broadened taste by adding new works to the repertoire of masterpieces and new concepts to the repertoire of aesthetics and philosophy; on consensus they have failed, however, to produce satisfying definitions of these period-styles, either as intellectual entities or as time-specific entities. That is, the student of mannerist literature or baroque science is left to ponder what meaningful unity may lie behind the five baroque categories of Heinrich Wölfflin or the eight baroque categories of Imbrie Buffum, or the like—as well as whether these categories may somehow have become operative at one point in time and ceased to be operative at another. Marcel Raymond writes, speaking of the mannerist style, that "il serait absurde de ranger toutes les oeuvres d'une même époque sous une même bannière" ["it would be absurd to line up all the works of an epoch under a single banner"]. And he thinks it similarly unreasonable that "un âge maniériste homogène aurait précédé un âge baroque homogène" ["a homogeneous mannerist age may have preceded a homogeneous baroque age"].[2]

What the great man, great age, and period-style approaches have in common, however, is a special notion of intellectual change. They assume, perhaps intuitively or even unconsciously, that the relative interest of different cultural moments is unequal and that the rate of intellectual change may somehow vary—now moving slowly through one of its great periods, now reaching a turning point, now plunging into some new configuration.

This possibly questionable but intuitively attractive assumption reappears, moreover, in the most modern accounts of intellectual movement, those based on the Saussurean linguistic notions of synchrony and diachrony. Such accounts—most notably Foucault in his *Les Mots et les choses* and other works—see intellectual movement, like Saussurean linguistic change, as a series of static, synchronic states succeeding each other in historical, diachronic time. In particular Foucault describes sudden, discontinuous movement, in the first two decades of the seventeenth century, from a complex of epistemological assumptions—an *épistémè*—based on the notions of resemblance, analogy, sympathy, and the like to an *épistémè* based on the notions of classification and representation, that is, from an epistemological stance perhaps best exemplified by Paracelsus to one perhaps best exemplified by Descartes.

Foucault himself has varied as to just how suddenly this occurred. And Foucault and writers like him have also been criticized for occasional lapses of time-specificity, for ignoring apparent counterexamples, and, especially, for leaving unexplained the causes of movement from one synchronic state to another. The semiotician A. J. Greimas, for example, has expressed regret that "une meilleure connaissance des règles générales de transformations structurelles est nécessaire avant qu'on puisse se prononcer avec quelque certitude sur le caractère spécifique des transformations diachroniques" ["a better understanding of the general rules of structural transformation is necessary before one can speak with assurance about the specific character of diachronic transformations"]. He adds that "il n'est pas du tout impossible qu'une certaine corrélation existe entre deux usages historiques successifs et disjoints: mais la méthodologie structuraliste ne semble pas, en tout cas, être en état, à l'heure actuelle, d'en préciser le status" ["it is not at all impossible that some correlation may exist between two successive and yet discontinuous historical usage systems: but structuralist methodology does not in any case appear to be in a position, as things stand now, to describe precisely its conditions"].[3]

Commenting on Foucault's description of successive, discontinuous states in Occidental thought—and certainly hoping to sketch out a more moderate or more eclectic position on intellectual change—Gilles Deleuze speculates that a superior model might be one of multiple series of sometimes independent, sometimes interacting states. These states would be sometimes stable, sometimes undergoing rapid transformation. Thus for Deleuze there may be various:

> seuils par exemple esthétiques, qui mobilisent un savoir dans une direction autre que celle d'une science, et qui permettraient de définir un texte littéraire, ou une oeuvre picturale, dans les pratiques discursives auxquelles elles appartiennent. Ou bien même des seuils éthiques, des seuils politiques: on montrerait comment des interdits, des exclusions, des limites, des libertés, des transgressions sont liées à une pratique discursive déterminée, en rapport avec des milieux non-discursifs, et plus ou moins aptes à s'approcher d'un seuil révolutionnaire. Ainsi se forme le poème-archéologie dans tous les registres de multiplicités, mais aussi dans l'unique inscription de ce qui est dit, en rapport avec les événements, les institutions et toutes les autres pratiques.

> [thresholds, perhaps aesthetic ones, which orient a body of knowledge in a different direction than that of a science, and which would allow a literary text or a pictural work to be defined according to discursive practices appropriate to it. Or perhaps there may be ethical thresholds, or political ones: one might show how the taboos, the exclusions, the limits, the liberties, and their transgressions are linked to a given discursive usage, related to non-discursive domains, and indeed more or less apt to approach a revolutionary threshold. Thus the archeological poem may be formed in all its registers and multiplicities, but also uniquely determined by what is said, in relation with the events, the institutions, and all the other practica].[4]

Just what such practices might be, of course, is not fully elucidated. One such description might be deduced, however, from Thomas S. Kuhn's well-known *Structure of Scientific Revolutions,* once described by Foucault himself as "admirable and definitive." Kuhn suggests that from time to time, in a given field of intellectual activity, the widely accepted "paradigm" of "normal" investigation may be troubled by unassimilable new facts. These anomalous facts may sometimes be so unsettling as to precipitate a crisis of explanation, then tinkering with the accepted theory, then more or less desperate invention of new theories to deal with the problem, and finally the success of one of these new theories, which becomes the paradigm of the following epoch. Kuhn's approach has the advantage of dealing effectively with irregular evolution (sometimes anomaly produces crisis, but sometimes researchers are simply willing to wait), with apparent counterexamples (always present in research), and the coexistence of apparently contradictory theories and styles (everyone casting about for new possibilities). Kuhn's account of scientific revolution synthesizes relatively formalistic and relatively more concrete empirical causes for intellectual change. As a semiempiricism, it is itself subject to various kinds of empirical tinkering. In any case, it is a model that tries to do justice—as does Deleuze's—to the intuitively perceived complexity and multiplicity of intellectual movement. As an account of scientific "revolution," it lends comfort also to the intuitive—or at least currently philosophically tempting— model of irregular intellectual movement and breakthrough susceptible to description on a structural model.[5]

Now it is a commonplace of these times that the structure of inquiry may largely determine the results—that any given method illuminates certain aspects of its subject and leaves others in shadow. The inverse corollary of this—and a seventeenth-century baroque idea as well—is that a variety of points of view, through their divergences, convergences, and possible mutual reinforcement, may give a relatively fuller and more complete description than any one alone. As Deleuze's statement quoted in the epigraph suggests, examples may lend themselves to a variety of approaches, methods, concepts, and conclusions. The results of any such eclectic inquiry should contribute both to understanding of the examples and to understanding of the movement of seventeenth-century thought.

It is another present-day commonplace, drawn from the repertoire of modern linguistics, that things have meaning only in comparison with other things. In this spirit, the following chapters compare nine pairs of texts to see how they lend themselves to analysis by a variety of methods and how those methods actually work themselves out in eighteen or more intellectual artifacts, dating from 1557 to 1719. These include two sonnets describing houses, two pessimistic dissertations on the thought process, two discussions of the nature of true love, two practical fencing manuals, two versions of a tragicomedy, two monologues on a particular moral dilemma, two mathematical treatises, two versions of the Phaedra legend, and two fables attacking superstition.

Some of these texts are obscure; others are widely celebrated masterpieces of the *Grand Siècle*. Although in the majority they are literary texts—a choice reflecting my own background and education—their bias and applicability are essentially unrelated to the notion of belles lettres. As recent exhaustive studies have shown, literary works represented only a fraction of the publishing and reading preoccupations of seventeenth-century France. The possibility of intellectual change, however, whether similar or divergent, extends into discourse of every kind. The texts chosen, therefore, are not so much tragedies, or novels, or manuals, or treatises as they are simply texts— that is, written objects.

In each case the resemblances will be numerous—resemblances of genre, subject, imagery, circumstance, vocabulary, and the like—informing pairs of objects comparable to any two madonnas, or Georgian candlesticks, or rococo perfume flasks, or any two Venus Anadyomenes of the *musée imaginaire*. The differences, possibly idiosyncratic, or trivial, or merely "historical" in some respects, may in others lend themselves to analysis of a variety of kinds. And the results of these analyses may be significant and, indeed, in some cases, convergent. Because of this the conclusions suggested—concrete and precise with respect to the particular texts studied in detail—may well be susceptible of extension to a variety of seventeenth-century discourse or even to seventeenth-century discourse in general.

Actually, at the price of some repetition, the present study might have been very long, treating seventeenth-century writing exhaustively according to the principles outlined here. Preliminary versions of the present work did in fact apply these same principles, with similar results, to a very different selection of texts. As it is, whether as vestiges of material not used or as projections of material that might have been developed in greater detail, the names of a great many prominent seventeenth-century writers and thinkers appear in the following pages.

Beginning well before the dawn of the seventeenth century and ending shortly after the death of Louis XIV, the examples and their extensions may hope to describe movement of seventeenth-century intellectual styles comparatively—that is, by comparison with what preceded and with what followed that period, as well as by comparison with nearer analogues.

Some readers may be displeased because the application methodology—or methodologies—is not coherent. That, of course, is precisely the idea. In something of the spirit of the Deleuze epigraph, I attempt to adopt an empirical or perhaps syncretic approach in the following pages. I will try less to adopt or exploit a given method than to see how various methods—in particular, but not at all exclusively those of Foucault and Kuhn—lend themselves to analysis of various texts. Or, conversely, how certain texts lend themselves to analysis by one or another method. As suggested above, the results may be convergent; they are, in any case, illuminating.

Some other readers may object that certain of the comparisons lead to rapid or even superficial treatment of difficult and much-studied intellectual issues. Given the very large body of writing and debate on aspects of seventeenth-century France, almost any textual comparison is likely to encounter—and fail to do justice to—important questions weighed carefully and subtly by specialists. Yet at the same time, if the results of inquiry depend on the point of view adopted, as the phenomenological cliché suggests, then any point of view at all—and particularly any view which may appear to simplify difficult and persistent questions—may hope to make a contribution to its subject. The apparent simplicity of certain descriptions, in any case, is not necessarily superficial or profound—and still less the result of any superior objectivity—but the result of the choice of a particular point of view.

It is my hope that this particular stance, that of a Deleuzian empirically minded reader seeking to study the application of various methods in divers texts, whatever its heuristic or intrinsic qualities, and whatever its concomitant problems, may nevertheless throw new light on long-standing problems of seventeenth-century intellectual change or, indeed, time-specific intellectual movement in general. In the end this approach may provide a particular style of reading for the vast body of seventeenth-century texts.

Such a reading style, rather than being reductive, may hope to illuminate an additional dimension of seventeenth-century writing—something like a "deep structure" or "cognitive dimension," in the current critical phrase—and in any case an epistemological dimension of seventeenth-century writing and thought.*

NOTES

1. Foucault, *Les Mots et les choses* (Paris: Gallimard, 1966), p. 7; Peyre, "Common-Sense Remarks on the French Baroque," in *Studies in Seventeenth-Century French Literature Presented to Morris Bishop* (Ithaca: Cornell University Press, 1962), pp. 5, 17, 18; Adam, *Histoire de la littérature française au XVIIe siècle* (Paris: Domat, 1956), 1: 584.

2. Marcel Raymond and A. J. Steele, eds., *La Poésie française et le maniérisme, 1546–1610 (?)* (Geneva: Droz, 1971), p. 5.

Some examples of problems in the "great age" approach may be found in such works as C. S. Lewis, *The Discarded Image* (Cambridge: Cambridge University Press, 1964), p. 13, or A. O. Lovejoy's *Great Chain of Being* (Cambridge: Harvard University Press, 1936), p. vii, or perhaps especially E. M. W. Tillyard's *Elizabethan World Picture* (New York: Macmillan, 1944). Tillyard writes, with

---

*The present work was in an advanced stage of preparation when Timothy J. Reiss published a powerful, related book, *The Discourse of Modernism* (Ithaca: Cornell University Press, 1982). I would prefer to reserve to some other place a fuller commentary on this very suggestive and important work.

Although Reiss seems not to mention Kuhn, he uses Kuhnian terminology to describe intellectual "revolution." He speaks extensively, for example, of "crisis" (e.g., pp. 9, 14) brought on by awareness of "internal contradictions" (p. 11) and "seemingly insoluble conflict" (p. 108) leading to intellectual change and then "consolidation" (p. 9).

In part for this reason, Reiss's book and the present work are complementary. Like the other authors adduced here, Reiss uses a different theoretical model and different examples. His results, however, are interestingly convergent. Reiss's discussion of "dominant occulted practice" and its deoccultation gains something from comparison to the present work's discussion of the opening of cognitive dimension and increased willingness to identify salient factors (Chapters 2 and 3). The present work's discussion of *Un Animal dans la lune* gains something from Reiss's exposition on the metaphor of the telescope. And so on.

self-awareness but also great casualness toward chronology, that "I sometimes use the word Elizabethan with great laxity, meaning anything within the compass of the English Renaissance, anything between the ages of Henry VIII and Charles I akin to the main trends of Elizabethan thought." Examples of more successfully chronological works may be Michael Macklem's *The Anatomy of the World: Relations between Natural and Moral Law from Donne to Pope* (Minneapolis: University of Minnesota Press, 1958), or Colin Martindale's *Romantic Progression* (Washington, D.C.: Hemisphere, 1975).

Meanwhile, bibliography of the mannerist and baroque styles is more than extensive: see C.-G. Dubois's *Le Baroque* (Paris: Larousse, 1973) for a recent extensive bibliography and René Wellek's "The Concept of the Baroque in Literature" with its relatively recent updating in his *Concepts of Criticism* (New Haven: Yale University Press, 1963).

At the same time, however, in the preface to *Le Baroque,* Dubois wonders whether the notion of baroque style, so much studied, is not now a little old hat. And even the author of a memorable book on *La Littérature de l'âge baroque en France* (Paris: Corti, 1954), Jean Rousset, writes in a later work that "Le temps est sans doute venu maintenant de s'en détourner [from the Baroque] et de passer outre" ["The time has no doubt come now to turn away (from the Baroque) and to move along"] (*L'Intérieur et l'extérieur* [Paris: Corti, 1968], p. 243).

As for reevaluation of French classicism, see not only the conclusion in the revised edition of Henri Peyre's *Qu' est-ce que le classicisme?* (Paris: Nizet, 1965), but also such works as E. B. O. Borgerhoff's *The Freedom of French Classicism* (Princeton: Princeton University Press, 1950); or even D. Mornet's *Histoire de la littérature française classique* (Paris: A. Colin, 1947); or the critical anthology edited by Jules Brody (himself an important contributor to the subject), *French Classicism* (New York: Prentice-Hall, 1966); or the Peyre commemoration number of the *Yale French Studies* devoted to *The Classical Line* (no. 38 [1967]); or the articles by Hugh M. Davidson and Robert J. Nelson published in the *Bucknell Review* (13 [1965], 37–62), or Nelson's more recent article, "The Bipolarity of French Classicism," in *EFL* (no. 8 [1971], 11–28), among others. Will G. Moore writes in his *French Classical Literature* ([London: Oxford University Press, 1961], p. 159) that his aim has been "to look afresh at the works of French literature usually known as classical, and to suggest that in the light of modern research they do not fit the categories to which they are by tradition assigned."

3. Greimas, *Du Sens* (Paris: Seuil, 1970), pp. 112, 113. The Marxian structuralist Louis Althusser asks rhetorically, "How is it possible to define the concept of a structural causality?" ("Marx's Immense Theoretical Revolution," reprinted in R. and F. de George, eds., *The Structuralists from Marx to Lévi-Strauss* [New York: Anchor, 1972], p. 245). A kind of answer can be found in an early

pronouncement by Roman Jakobson and J. Tynianov, who asserted that "The history of a system is in turn also a system ("Problems in the Study of Language and Literature," ibid., p. 82). Unfortunately, such a statement returns to the view that nothing really ever changes, since everything would then be contained in a Jakobsonian metastructure, slowly unfolding like the miracle of God's eternal creation (but see F. W. Galan, "Literary System and Systemic Change: The Prague School Theory of Literary History, 1928-48," *PMLA* 94 [1979], 275-85). As Roland Barthes writes, moreover, any such system has the weakness of representing "the historical process as a pure succession of forms" ("The Structuralist Activity," in De George, eds., *The Structuralists,* p. 148). See also Jeffrey Mehlman, who hopes for a "structural history" in his *A Structural Study of Autobiography* (New Haven: Yale University Press, 1971), p. 13, etc.

Jean Piaget criticizes Foucault at length in *Structuralism* (London: Routledge, 1971), pp. 51, 128-35, 142. Piaget has himself tried to develop a theory of intellectual change based on the insights of his study of the psychological development of children. Piaget writes that "les lois psychologiques obtenues grâce à notre méthode se prolongent en lois épistémologiques . . . l'élimination du réalisme, du substantivisme, du dynamisme, les progrès du relativisme, etc., sont autant de lois d'évolution qui paraissent communes à l'évolution de l'enfant et au développement de la réflexion scientifique" ["the psychological laws obtained through our method may be extended to become epistemological laws . . . the elimination of realism, of substantivism, or dynamism, the progress of relativism, etc., are so many laws of evolution which appear to be common to the evolution of the child and the development of scientific reflection"] (*La Causalité physique chez l'enfant* [Paris: F. Alcan, 1927], pp. 272-73). For other negative discussions of Foucault, see Jean Baudrillard's *Oublier Foucault* (Paris: Galilée, 1977) and Karlis Racevskis's *Michel Foucault and the Subversion of Intellect* (Ithaca: Cornell University Press, 1983).

Students of synchrony and diachrony are sometimes no more precise chronologically than the students of great ages. For example, in a phrase reminiscent of Tillyard, the relatively much more modern Noam Chomsky readily apologizes in the preface of his fascinating *Cartesian Linguistics* because "this will be something of a composite portrait. There is no single individual who can be shown to have held all the views that will be sketched." Chomsky adds that "Descartes himself devoted little attention to language" and that if any individual is characteristic of "Cartesian linguistics" it is less Descartes than "perhaps Humboldt" ([New York: Harper & Row, 1966], p. 2).

4. Deleuze, *Un Nouvel Archiviste* (Montpellier: Fata Morgana, 1972), p. 44.

5. Kuhn, *The Structure of Scientific Revolutions* (Chicago: University of Chicago Press, 1962). Foucault, in "Foucault Responds/2," *Diacritics* 1 (1971), 60.

For commentary on Kuhn, see Gary Gutting, ed., *Paradigms and Revolutions*

(South Bend: Notre Dame University Press, 1980), especially Alasdair MacIntyre, "Epistemological Crises, Dramatic Narrative, and the Philosophy of Science," who describes Hamlet, more or less contemporary with texts discussed in the following pages, in terms of "epistemological crisis" (pp. 54–74).

Two Descriptive Sonnets: Du Bellay's
Anet and Ronsard's Saint-Cosme

A FUNDAMENTAL FUNCTION of literature has probably always been the description of the world. Any extensive anthology of sixteenth- and seventeenth-century French poetry—like that of other periods—might be expected to contain any number of poems enumerating the qualities of beloved ladies or kings or princes or divers patrons. It would also contain descriptions of creations of nature, of the works of man, and all manner of objects, animate and inanimate. The collections of some imaginary museum or flea market of antique French poetry might offer the empiricist any number of coy mistresses or Petrarchian madonnas or *blasons* of feminine body parts or royal personages or precious stones or indeed such apparently capricious descriptions as Rémy Belleau's *Huître* or Aubert's *Ciron* or the great Ronsard's *Alouette* or *Salade* or *Grenouille* or the satyric Sigogne's courtier's *Nez* or the libertine Saint-Amant's *Melon* or *Cidre* or *Fromage,* among hundreds or indeed thousands of other poetic artifacts of the period. And, whatever dissatisfaction might be expressed with the various definitions of these literary period styles, each one would fit in one way or another into Renaissance or mannerist or baroque or precious or burlesque styles, as variously defined by one or another of the writers on the subject.

In this period of possibly very diverse poetic description, the force of poetic tradition was nevertheless such that almost any given word, motif, proverbial wisdom, or ironic wordplay might seemingly—like the hands, the eyes, or the decorative garlands in paintings or engravings of the same period—be repeated in a variety of poetic or aesthetic contexts. For this reason, critical editions of such works are sometimes a hodgepodge of more or less trivial-appearing half-sources and minor resemblances. For works in this genre in particular, literary history rarely provides precise and dependable information about the date and circumstances of composition of individual pieces. Most often such poems are thought to have been recited or sung or circulated in manuscript(s)—typically poorly dated—for indefinite periods before being printed in books bearing a date of publication. Classic principles of information theory suggest that relatively long poems should be easier to date and situate from internal evidence; relatively short poems, however, as they select, embroider, vary, and rearrange elements within a limited poetic tradition, may appear more similar than different to a twentieth-century reader. Like the ironmongery or unread clay tablets of ancient civilizations, such works may appear difficult to date or situate in more than rather general terms.

Such might at first appear to be the case also for two sixteenth-century French sonnets which, as it happens, can be dated by external evidence to within a few years or a few months—a description of the château of Anet by Du Bellay, first published in 1558 and apparently composed in 1557, and a description of a humbler residence written by Ronsard on the occasion of a royal visit, in August or September of 1576. Describing a building completed in 1552 and variously described by specialists as an outstanding example of classical—or, according to some, mannerist—architecture, Du Bellay writes, addressing the château's owner, Diane de Poitiers:

> De vostre Dianet—de vostre nom j'appelle
> Vostre maison d'Anet—la belle architecture,
> Les marbres animez, la vivante peinture,
> Qui la font estimer des maisons la plus belle:
>   Les beaux lambriz dorez, la luisante chappelle,
> Les superbes dongeons, la riche couverture,
> Le jardin tapissé d'éternelle verdure,
> Et la vive fonteine à la source immortelle:
>   Ces ouvrages, Madame, à qui bien les contemple,
> Rapportant de l'antiq' le plus parfait exemple,
> Monstrent un artifice, et despense admirable.
>   Mais ceste grand' doulceur jointe à ceste haultesse,
> Et cest Astre benin joint à ceste sagesse,
> Trop plus que tout cela vous font emerveillable.

[In your Dianette—for I call your house of Anet by your own name—the beautiful architecture, the animate marbles, the living paintings, which cause it to be judged the most beautiful of houses: the beautiful gilded panels, the shining chapel, the magnificent keep, the rich covering, the garden carpeted with eternal greenery, and the sparkling fountain with its immortal spring.

These works, Madam, to whoever contemplates them, bringing back from antiquity its most perfect example, show admirable and lavish artifice. But your great goodness, joined with your haughty manner, and that benign star joined with your wisdom, even more than all that render you worthy of marvel.]

Welcoming Henri III's brother François de Valois, duke of Touraine, to his romanesque priory, Saint-Cosme, Ronsard wrote some twenty years later in 1576 that:

> Bien que ceste maison ne vante son porphire,
> Son marbre ny son jaspe en oeuvre elabouré:
> Que son plancher ne soit lambrissé ny doré,
> Ny portrait de tableaux que le vulgaire admire:
>   Toutefois Amphion l'a bien daigné construire,
> Où le son de sa lyre est encor demeuré,
> Où Phoebus comme en Delphe y est seul honoré,
> Où la plus belle Muse a choisi son Empire.
>   Apprenez, mon grand Prince, à mespriser les biens,
> La richesse d'un Prince est l'amitié des siens:
> Le reste des grandeurs nous abuse et nous trompe.
>   La bonté, la vertu, la justice, et les lois
> Aiment mieux bien souvent les antres et les bois,
> Que l'orgueil des Palais, qui n'ont rien que la pompe.

[Although this house cannot boast porphyry, nor marble nor jasper worked into elaborate form; although its planks are neither paneled nor gilded, and it has no portrait or picture for the vulgar to admire; even so, Amphion indeed did deign to build it, in which the sound of his lyre still remains, where Phoebus as in Delphi is alone honored, where the most beautiful muse has chosen her domain. Learn, my great Prince, to scorn material goods; the wealth of a prince is the friendship of his clan; the remaining part of worldly grandeur abuses and tricks us. Goodness, virtue, justice, and the laws often prefer caverns and forest to the pride of palaces, which have nothing but pomp].[1]

The two residences described are very different; at the same time, however, the two descriptions employ—positively or negatively—very similar elements. Both the Renaissance castle and the Romanesque priory are called "maison" in the initial line of their respective sonnets. Both poems, in the presumably more or less obligatory enumeration of decorative features and parts that follows, mention marble—whether

14

the "marbres animez" of Anet or the marble, jasper, and porphyry that are absent from Saint-Cosme. In the same way Du Bellay's Anet offers examples of a "vivante peinture" and "beaux lambriz dorez," while Ronsard's more humble residence, in his description, has "Ny portrait de tableaux que le vulgaire admire" nor a ceiling that is "lambrissé ny doré."

Both sonnets contain suggestions of structure, whether the "belle architecture" of Anet or its numerous remarkable "ouvrages," or Ronsard's nonexistent marble and jasper "en oeuvre élabouré." Both texts use numerous superlatives and terms of high praise and do so in ways which lend themselves to varying interpretations. Any such ornaments may be simply a rhetorical necessity of the subject and the genre or may possibly suggest mannerist paradox or *meriviglie,* or perhaps Imbrie Buffum's baroque category of "emphasis and exaggeration." Thus Du Bellay describes a castle which is of all castles "la plus belle," surrounded by eternal greenery and provided with a "source immortelle." Du Bellay's Anet, moreover, is "le plus parfait exemple" of the antique—presumably a reference to Anet's very pure classical or, according to another view, highly intellectualized and mannerist—architectural style. In the same way, Ronsard's Saint-Cosme is a place where Apollo is "seul honoré," a house inhabited by "la plus belle Muse."[2]

As the last image implies, moreover, both sonnets contain suggestions—possibly Renaissance or mannerist or baroque or timeless ones—of magical or mythological presences. Thus Du Bellay freely personifies, for laudatory effect, Anet's marbles, which are animated, as well as its "vivante" painting. In something like a mannerist—or baroque—love of artifice, Anet's chapel is "luisante," its keeps are "superbes," and its gardens are, as the poetic convention has it, "tapissé," or carpeted, with an astonishingly and perhaps magically "éternelle verdure." Similarly, Anet's "vive fonteine" taps an immortal spring. In an example that, like those of Du Bellay, would fit Buffum's baroque category of "incarnation," Ronsard personifies his house, which cannot *vanter,* or boast decorations of exotic stone. At the same time, its very construction is magical or mythological, and it is otherwise associated with Apollo, Delphi, and the muse.

Both sonnets, of course, turn at a certain point from architectural description to personal description—whether of a stellar owner or a royal visitor—and new superlatives, terms of high praise, incarnations, and mythological allusions appear. Having addressed Diane de Poitiers in the second person in the sonnet's initial line, Du Bellay turns in the last tercet to "ceste grand' doulceur," that is, Diane's, and to her "haultesse." Momentarily confounding Diane de Poitiers with her mythological namesake, Du Bellay evokes the goddess Diana's attributes, her "Astre benin" and her "sagesse." In the *pointe* which closes the sonnet, all these good qualities make Diane de Poitiers more "émerveillable" even than the multiple splendors of her castle Anet. Meanwhile, the last six lines of Ronsard's poem praise the duke—like the priory—in an indirect or even backward manner. In this section of the sonnet Ronsard delivers a kind of moral homily to "mon grand Prince." A prince should learn to scorn riches; his true wealth is "l'amitié des siens." Anything else, any of the "reste des grandeurs," is illusory. Just as illusory, as Ronsard suggests in his own final *pointe,* is "l'orgueil des Palais, qui n'ont rien que la pompe."

If the elements which are common to both sonnets are subject to varying interpretations in light of the various stylistic systems that may be applied to sixteenth- and seventeenth-century French poetry, the differences between the two poems may appear similarly inconclusive. In the absence of that specific information which happens to allow dating of these two texts, any but the boldest or most intuitive empiricist might hesitate to assign dates or stylistic labels—or perhaps even chronological priority—to them. For example, Du Bellay's sonnet begins with a play on words: "Dianet." And the author himself somewhat laboriously points out in the following line and a half what the wordplay means: this diminutive form of Diane's name contains the name of her château. No equivalent wordplay and explanation appear in the Ronsard poem. Now, if the explanation might be taken by some as an example of classical reason, the play on words itself and the sonnet's concluding *pointe* and so on might be taken by others as mannerist traits. In the same way, if Du Bellay's compliment suggesting that Anet represents "de l'antiq' le plus parfait exemple" may imply allegiance to the classical ideal, his other suggestion that Anet shows "un artifice" and indeed a "despense admirable" might suggest a more perverse—or mannerist—esthetic. Some might draw similar conclusions from the "part-oriented" enumeration of Anet's various beauties, or Du Bellay's "florid" style, his personifications, or his superlatives, or his possible air of refined detachment toward the subject. At the same time, meanwhile, some of the traits listed above are among those—Du Bellay's superlatives, his incarnations, and the like—that are claimed in common by both mannerist and baroque definitions commonly proposed.

Similarly, Ronsard's architectural sonnet also contains traits associated with mannerist or baroque styles—including some claimed jointly, so to speak, by a variety of proposed stylistic definitions. As quoted above, the first quatrain of Ronsard's sonnet also presents an enumeration of possibly mannerist *meriviglie,* and his second offers a more extensive and more elaborate mythological repertory than Du Bellay's. Whether or not Ronsard may have believed more sincerely—or insincerely—than Du Bellay in the world of mythological allusion, he adds to Apollo, Delphi, and the muse already cited the mythological figure of Amphion. It is Amphion, said to have constructed the city of Thebes magically by playing his three-stringed lyre, who has also "bien daigné construire" Ronsard's house at Saint-Cosme. For Buffum, such a suggestion might be not only an example of baroque theatricality but also a more special kind of baroque incarnation. For Amphion, the mysterious and hence semisupernatural figure of mythology, thus not only deigns to perform tasks worthy of him, that is, tasks rooted in the world of classic myth, but also tasks of a more humble and everyday kind—the construction of Ronsard's very humble, unornamented, and ordinary cottage. If in such an allusion the gods (or mythological figures somewhat like them) are made to come down to earth to perform everyday work, something like the reverse is also true. Not only has Amphion constructed Ronsard's house, but "le son de sa lyre est encor demeuré" therein, thus divinizing a humble and very terrestrial place.

Such high praise of poetry, moreover, might suggest something like the mental stage of intellectual substantivism posited by Jean Piaget as one of those configurations of thought through which the developing mind must pass before reaching maturity. And if the first tercet might suggest Renaissance simplicity in its appeal to the "amitié des siens" or its warning that "Le reste des grandeurs nous abuse & nous trompe," the final tercet might be taken as an apology for Michel Foucault's *épistémè* of resemblance. For in the last section Ronsard suggests that such notions as "La bonté, la vertu, la justice & les lois" are creations of nature rather than of man, preferring "bien souvent les antres & les bois" to "l'orgueil des Palais, qui n'ont rien que la pompe."

Taken as wholes and on consensus of the various definitions offered, Du Bellay's sonnet contains a preponderance of classical and mannerist elements, while Ronsard's sonnet contains a preponderance of mannerist and baroque elements—possibly a pleasing conclusion, since such a view appears to correspond "correctly" to the chronological situation. Yet, as a general proposition, it might seem unlikely that any sixteenth-century evolution through classical, mannerist, and baroque styles might proceed, like a precisely disciplined chemical reaction, in an orderly and regular proportional movement. To such a model, one might even prefer Arnold Hauser's somewhat cumbersome and confusing remark that "some critics explain mannerism as a reaction against the early baroque, and the high baroque as a counter-movement which then superseded mannerism again. In that case the history of sixteenth-century art would turn on a repeated clash between the baroque and mannerism, with initial success going to the latter and final victory to the former." But at the same time the apparently rather free commingling of elements suggestive of different styles in these two sonnets might better lend confirmation to Marcel Raymond's very rightly skeptical doubts, already quoted, that between 1520 and 1600 or later any "âge maniériste homogène aurait précédé un âge baroque homogène" ["homogeneous mannerist age might have preceded a homogeneous baroque age"]. More reasonably, the two sonnets studied here confirm Raymond's empirical impression that "des éléments maniéristes et baroques composent ensemble, s'interpénètrent, chez un même peintre, dans un même tableau, a fortiori chez un même poète. Dans un poème donné, ces éléments, qui seront rarement tous réunis et convergents, pourront même laisser dans le doute, quant à leur appartenance maniériste ou baroque" ["mannerist and baroque elements come to terms with each other, mingle together in a single painter, in a single picture, a fortiori in a single poet. In a given poem these elements, which are rarely all united and convergent, may even leave some doubt as to whether they belong to mannerism or baroque"].[3]

THE PRECEDING ANALYSIS is itself something like a summary of the controversies, problems, and uncertainties surrounding varying definitions of mannerist and baroque styles — or indeed the problem of diachronic stylistic change in general. Some light may be shed on the matter, however, if Du Bellay's and Ronsard's sonnets are reanalyzed according to a criterion not usually associated with these stylistic notions. Sonnets generally — and especially poetic occasional pieces like the Du Bellay and Ronsard sonnets quoted here — are rarely, if ever, considered to be vehicles of philosophical speculation; yet it remains a curious and striking fact that both texts contain a remarkable body of statement

18

concerning the ways in which knowledge is organized and hence, ultimately, the ways in which the world may be organized.

In the Du Bellay sonnet, for example, the first line's play on words contains the word "nom," that is, the divinely or humanly assigned designation which permits objects or concepts to be manipulated in the abstract. The first line also contains the verb "j'appelle," that is, the act of assigning or using names and, inevitably, limiting and sorting out the resemblances and differences, the categories and allegiances of the world. Elsewhere in Du Bellay's sonnet appear the words "estimer," "contemple," "rapportant" (in a sense implying a "bringing back" from antiquity, but also a choice of and selection within antique architectural style), the verb "monstrent," the noun "artifice" (in the possibly rather special sense of the ability to fabricate unreality from reality, structure from things unstructured), the adjective "admirable," the participles "jointe" and "joint," the noun "sagesse," and the final adjective "émerveillable."

In the text each of these words has the effect not only of presenting the world—Anet, its fountains, Diane de Poitiers—but also of placing each item in a specifically definable intellectual context. The same is true of most if not all of the supposedly mannerist or baroque traits summarized above, since each one, certainly, can be interpreted as one form of "distancing" the description from the subject, or one way of calling attention to aspects of the subject. Thus the mannerist or baroque superlatives have the effect of calling attention to extreme qualities. Both the mannerist *pointes* and the baroque incarnations have the effect of bringing together objects usually thought to belong to very different ontological domains—celestial and terrestrial concerns—or the beauty of houses and that of their owners. The effect, presumably, is to move reflection out of its usual patterns, to stimulate reflection of some new and different kind. As Foucault writes, "On sait ce qu'il y a de déconcertant dans la proximité des extrêmes ou tout bonnement dans le voisinage soudain des choses sans rapport; l'énumération qui les entrechoque possède à elle seule un pouvoir d'enchantement" ["Everyone knows what is disconcerting about the proximity of extremes, or indeed in the sudden juxtaposition of unrelated things; the enumeration which throws them together itself possesses a power of enchantment"].[4]

Taken together, the "knowledge-related" words enumerated above make up twelve of 103 words, or about 12 percent of the total. From a slightly different point of view, the same twelve words make up twenty-six of 168 syllables in the sonnet, or some 15 percent. The addition of superlatives, incarnations, and other mannerist or baroque traits would, of course, increase such quantitative findings.

Ronsard's description of Saint-Cosme similarly contains terms suggesting modes of knowledge and structuration. Thus Ronsard writes that his house may not "vante" its porphyry and that its marble and jasper are not "en oeuvre elabouré." His house has neither "portrait" nor "tableaux," that is, representations of reality, which a vulgar person may "admire." In the second quatrain the reader learns that Amphion has not only constructed this dwelling, but he has also "daigné [le] construire." Amphion's specifically poetic attribute, the "son de sa lyre," has remained in the house, moreover. Similarly "honoré[s]" in the house are "Phoebus," the god of poetry, and "Delphe," the oracle famous in antiquity and in seventeenth-century literature for the generation of ambiguous truth. Another inhabitant is a "Muse," indeed the most beautiful one, who has "choisi" the house for the exercise of her authority or "Empire." In the tercets Ronsard's royal visitor is exhorted to "apprenez" true wisdom and to scorn, or "mespriser," worldly goods, which, with other worldly grandeurs "abuse[nt]" and deceive, or "trompe[nt]." Ronsard also presents a series of abstractions, used habitually by philosophers to organize moral and other knowledge: "La bonté, la vertu, la justice & les lois." He asserts that these abstractions, as personified in the text, "aiment mieux" a natural or bucolic setting, as opposed to the "orgueil" and the "pompe" of manmade palaces.

The words just quoted from Ronsard's poem total a possibly surprising twenty-eight of 123 words, or some 23 percent. Taken as syllables, the words quoted above represent fifty-two of 168 syllables, or a possibly astonishing 31 percent. Addition of various superlatives, incarnations, *pointes,* and the like would increase the total further.

Now whatever may or may not be the implicit epistemological message of Du Bellay's or Ronsard's architectural description, it is clear that words of an epistemologically categorizing sort make up a significant portion of their content. Moreover, for no immediately obvious reason, they make up something like twice as much of the Ronsard sonnet as of the very strikingly similar sonnet by Du Bellay. Both poems describe and praise houses, ladies, virtues, and mythological entities; both sonnets mention similar features and use strikingly similar vocabulary; both sonnets make room for the vocabulary of epistemological statement —but the later sonnet approximately twice as much as the earlier.

Within the narrow context of these two sixteenth-century French poems, a very wide range of traits that have been identified with mannerist or baroque styles appear not as the supposed decadence of a classicizing civilization—nor indeed as an ultimately meaningless enchantment with *maniera* for its own sake—but as a preoccupation, and indeed an increasing preoccupation, with the conditions of knowledge. Just as the greater interest in painterly, or chiaroscuro, or atmospheric effects in Heinrich Wölfflin's famous definition of baroque style may suggest an increasing interest in the conditions of vision, so greater preoccupation with verbal effect, with figures that call into question the relationship between things, and with the conditions of knowledge itself may appear to characterize both mannerist and baroque elements in these two artifacts of the latter half of the sixteenth century. Taken together, these elements constitute something like an epistemological dimension of discourse—so that both poems everywhere present not only images and information but also references to the conditions under which that information may be understood. As such, in addition to any scanty hints they may give about Piagetian substantivism or Foucaldian resemblance, they may also suggest something like a developing crisis in thought of the kind described by Thomas S. Kuhn—a crisis which, in the sciences or in philosophy or epistemology might have preceded any so-called Cartesian revolution.

ONE MIGHT WONDER to what extent such analysis of these two very short poems might be extended to other works from the same period. Presumably, if the epistemologizing vocabulary of these texts is in some sense supported by their superlatives and incarnations, one might look for similar support in other works from other tendencies associated with mannerist and baroque styles—the "distant" or contrived metaphors or the *métaphore filée* or the conceits or the oxymoron, all also sometimes thought to be characteristic of these period styles—along with baroque horror, or baroque theatricality, or surprise, or the like. For in other texts also, each of these may have the effect of calling attention to the artificial nature of the information presented—as well as to the manner of its presentation.

At the same time the hypotheses developed above to deal with a very limited sample may also find confirmation in more comprehensive studies of late sixteenth- and early seventeenth-century poetry. The extensive repertoire of examples in André Baîche's recent study of *La*

Naissance du baroque largely neglects the vocabulary of cognition but shows a marked increase in the vocabulary of perception in such poets as Du Bartas and D'Aubigné. The suggestions made above might seem to confirm Baîche's view that, beginning in the time of Desportes and D'Aubigné, "L'intellect gouverne la poésie: état de fait annonciateur des salons de préciosité" ["Intellect governs poetry: a state of affairs which announces the precious salons"]. Similarly, the suggestions made above would appear to find confirmation in John Pedersen's fascinating and excellent study of certain *Images et figures dans la poésie de l'âge baroque.* In particular, his work concludes that evolution of poetic imagery from the sixteenth to the seventeenth centuries may be based preponderantly on "des rapprochements parfois très surprenants produits par la création de nouveaux rapports" ["sometimes very surprising rapprochements produced by the creation of new relationships"] and that other images may be best understood "comme des signes, plutôt que comme des reproductions de la réalité" ["as signs, rather than as reproductions of reality"]. Finally, in his remarkable *Formes métaphoriques dans la poésie lyrique de l'âge baroque en France,* Fernand Hallyn similarly sees a movement in poetic imagery, attested in a very wide variety of texts, from the reproduction of "les combinaisons et les correspondances données dans la nature" ["the combinations and correspondences given in nature"] to "une activité pareille à celle de Dieu en établissant dans l'art des combinaisons et des correspondances *neuves,* en créant quelque chose qui soit sans précédent dans la nature" ["an activity like God's activity as it establishes something without precedent in nature"].[5]

THERE WILL BE much more to say about this in subsequent pages, particularly with respect to the relative importance of art over nature, apropos of other intellectual artifacts. For the present, however, a single additional example may be suggestive. For the French poetic tradition provides at least one other sonnet of architectural description in the same vein as Du Bellay's and Ronsard's. This is the poetic reformer Malherbe's famous description of Fontainebleau, apparently dating from a visit Malherbe made there in June 1607, some fifty years after Du Bellay described Anet and some thirty years after Ronsard received the duke of Touraine at Saint-Cosme. Although neither Du Bellay's poem nor Ronsard's is usually cited as a source of Malherbe's sonnet, the similarities are striking, so that Malherbe's text seems almost a conflation of the other two:

Beaux et grands bastimens d'éternelle structure,
Superbes de matiere et d'ouvrages divers,
Où le plus digne Roy qui soit en l'Univers
Aux miracles de l'Art fait ceder la Nature.
Beau Parc, et beaux Jardins, qui dans vostre closture,
Avez tousjours des fleurs, et des ombrages vers,
Non sans quelque Demon qui deffend aux hyvers
D'en effacer jamais l'agreable peinture.
Lieux qui donnez aux coeurs tant d'aimables desirs,
Bois, fontaines, canaux, si parmy vos plaisirs
Mon humeur est chagrine, et mon visage triste:
Ce n'est point qu'en effet vous n'ayez des appas,
Mais, quoy que vous ayez, vous n'avez point Caliste:
Et moy je ne voy rien quand je ne la voy pas.

[Beautiful and great buildings of eternal structure, superb in mate-
rials and in diverse works, where the most worthy king of all the
universe makes nature give way to the miracles of art; beautiful
park and beautiful gardens, which in your enclosure always have
flowers and green shadows, not to mention some demon who forbids the winters ever to erase your pleasant tableau; sites which
give to hearts so many loving desires—woods, fountains, canals, if
among your pleasures my mood is one of disappointment, and my
face sad, it is not that in reality you do not have charms, but
whatever you have, you do not have Caliste, and I see nothing
when I see her not].[6]

Malherbe's poem is included in Raymond's anthology of *La Poésie
française et le maniérisme, 1546–1610 (?)*, in his section on "La Louange et
la fête." Judging by the criteria presented in his own introduction, the
editor presumably admires the poem's decentered or compartmental-
ized structure and its final *pointe,* as well as the work's energetic or
"floride" style, all qualities which it has in common with Du Bellay's
and Ronsard's sonnets. A student of the baroque style, moreover, might
appreciate especially the ostentatious "facade" of Malherbe's "Beaux et
grands bastimens," his superlatives, his incarnate demon, his contrasts,
his possibly surprising ending, and so on. At the same time, a similar
count of epistemologically oriented words (e.g., "beaux," "structure,"
"superbes de matiere," "ouvrages," "miracles," "art") gives something
like twenty-seven words out of 123, or approximately 22 percent—or
some forty-six of 168 syllables, about 27 percent. If statistics of this kind
suggest an increased epistemological preoccupation in Ronsard's sonnet,

then they should suggest a continuing epistemological preoccupation—or uncertainty or perhaps Kuhnian paradigmatic crisis in Malherbe's.

Even with the addition of a third sonnet—or a fourth or a fifth—the sample studied here will or would remain extremely small. Within that small but enlarged sample, however, the various elements continue to behave in the same manner. Analysis of these texts in terms of the various definitions of mannerist or baroque style remains instructive but inconclusive—like the definitions themselves—not only because elements of each intermingle in the texts, but also because the definitions themselves have numerous elements in common. At the same time the later texts seem to reflect increased preoccupation with the conditions of knowledge, as evidenced by very significant proportions of epistemologically categorizing words—with whatever supporting figures, *pointes,* superlatives, incarnations, and the like that an empirically minded reader may wish to include in any such epistemologically oriented reading.

The Malherbe sonnet, like its predecessors, contains some relatively more explicit commentary on the conditions of verbal descriptions, moreover. Du Bellay's sonnet speaks of "artifice," which may fit one or more of the various definitions of mannerist style; it also speaks of some "plus parfait exemple" of the antique—and hence perhaps purely classical—style. Ronsard's sonnet suggests that justice and law are creatures of nature rather than of man. Malherbe's sonnet also makes statements on issues of this kind. In something like what Hauser sees as the unifying or structuring principle of baroque style as opposed to mannerist multiplicity, Malherbe speaks of the "éternelle structure" of Fontainebleau or the "plus digne Roy qui soit en l'Univers" or the "closture" and presumably un-baroque constancy of Fontainebleau's gardens, "tousjours" provided with flowers and "jamais" without their "agreable peinture." More specifically—and whether in the service of mannerist artifice, as Raymond may have believed, or of some other aesthetic or epistemological consideration—Malherbe writes that in Fontainebleau the universe's most worthy king "Aux miracles de l'Art fait ceder la Nature."

The possible supremacy of nature or human artifice would be an issue, of course, in any possible Cartesian or Foucaldian transformation of epistemological or epistemic preoccupations. This issue is already implied in Ronsard's view of naturalistic justice and law, as well as in a variety of other texts in the period. Malherbe's 1607 sonnet, in contrast, represents a Cartesian or Foucaldian representational position. A variety of later seventeenth-century texts take a variety of views on this fundamental epistemological issue, as the succeeding chapters suggest.

N O T E S

1. Du Bellay, *Poètes du XVIe siècle*, ed. A. M. Schmidt (Paris: Pléiade, 1953), p. 508; Ronsard, *Oeuvres complètes*, ed. P. Laumonnier and I. Silver, 17 (Paris: Didier, 1959), pp. 341–42.

2. The bibliography on this subject is so extensive as to merit a specialized bibliography of its own (for example, in Dubois, *Le Baroque*, pp. 247–56). But see especially J. Shearman, *Mannerism* (Harmondsworth: Penguin, 1967); Arnold Hauser, *Mannerisim* (London: Routledge, 1965); Raymond and Steele, eds., *La Poésie française et le maniérisme;* Imbrie Buffum, *Studies in the Baroque* (New Haven: Yale University Press, 1957); Rousset, *La Littérature de l'âge baroque en France;* and chapter 1 herein.

3. Hauser, *Mannerism*, p. 20; Raymond and Steele, p. 5.

4. Foucault, *Les Mots et les choses*, p. 8.

5. Baîche, *La Naissance du baroque* (Lille: Svc. reprod. thèses, 1973), p. 153, and his repertoire; Pedersen, *Images et figures*...(Copenhagen: Akademisk, 1974), p. 221; Hallyn, *Formes metaphoriques dans la poésie lyrique*...(Geneva: Droz, 1975). See also Rousset, "La querelle de la métaphore," in *Intérieur et l'extérieur*, pp. 57–71.

6. Malherbe in Raymond and Steele, p. 155. For two other examples, see Scarron's parody (in *Anthologie de la poésie française. XVIIe siècle*, 2 ([Paris: Garnier-Flammarion, 1966], p. 87) and a poem by Benserade (ibid., pp. 123–24).

CHAPTER 3

Two Images of the Thought Process:
Montaigne's *Essais* and
Charron's *De la sagesse*

LOGICALLY, enunciation precedes the *énoncé*. The process of thinking precedes the product of thought. And while late sixteenth- and early seventeenth-century authors use the vocabulary of epistemology to espouse varying doctrines of knowledge, the same authors show a possibly surprising unanimity in their description of the act of thinking itself. While the texts express quibbling and controversy as to the nature and usefulness of reason, imagination, language, memory, and judgment, the same texts agree that the thought process is complicated, confusing, wearying, uncertain, and unrewarding. The baroque theme of ceaseless flux and movement extends to activity inside the human head.

The following pages will study some serious-minded, even pedantic pronouncements of the philosophers on this subject; the most striking characterizations, however, come from a variety of poets. Among the latter, the baroque or mannerist Philippe Desportes wrote sometime before 1569 that

> Les pensers des hommes ressemblent
> A l'air, aux vents, et aux saisons,
> Et aux girouettes qui tremblent
> Inconstamment sur les maisons.
>   Leur amour est ferme et constante
> Comme la mer grosse de flots,
> Qui bruit, qui court, qui se tourmante,
> Et jamais n'arreste en repos.
>   Ce n'est que vent que de leur teste,
> De vent est leur entendement:
> Les vents encore et la tempeste
> Ne vont pas si legerement.

[The thoughts of men resemble the air, the winds, the seasons, and the weather-vanes that tremble erratically above the houses. Their love is firm and constant like the high seas' waves, which sound, which run, which boil, and never stop to rest. Their heads are only wind, and only wind their understanding; indeed the winds and the tempest do not go so lightly.]

Returning to this subject in another poem, written sometime before 1583, Desportes evokes:

> Mon prompt et peu sage penser,
> Qui peut haut et bas s'élancer,
> Et se feint cent formes nouvelles,

[My prompt and not very wise thought, which can jump high or low and play at a hundred new forms].

Really fecund in this kind of image, Desportes cries out elsewhere against a "vain penser! ô folle outrecuidance," laments a "miserable esprit," or "mes pensers variables," or "Mes pensers importuns," "ses pensers inconstans," or "Pensers, desirs, soucis pleins d'importunité," various "Espoirs, songes, pensers l'un à l'autre accrochant," or the poet's "lasches pensers," as well as "Mille debats confus" which "agitent ma pensée." Desportes evokes a "lict à mes pensers . . . un champ de bataille." He laments characteristically, "Ah Dieu! que de pensers tournent dedans ma teste!" He confides that "J'ay mille autres pensers, et mille et mille et mille,/Qui font qu'incessamment mon esprit se distile" ["I have a thousand other thoughts, and a thousand and a thousand and a thousand, which make my head incessantly sweat"].[1]

In much the same way Desportes's sometime adversary, Malherbe, writes in early poems of a "penser incertain" (1575), of his "fragiles pensées" (1587), of a "lasche pensée" (1587), and the like. Elsewhere, the preclassical reformer apostrophizes:

> Laisse moy raison importune,
> Cesse d'affliger mon repos,
> En me faisant mal à propos
> Desesperer de ma fortune.

[Leave me, importunate reason, cease to trouble my repose, making me at the wrong time despair of my fortunes—1606 or 1607].

Like Desportes, Malherbe evokes the sea which, in a no doubt baroque comparison with the act of thought, "a moins de vents qui ses vagues irritent,/Que je n'ay de pensers qui tous me solicitent" ["has fewer winds to irritate its wave than I have thoughts which all cry out to me"—1609]. Similar images and similar complaints are frequent in poems by the satyrical Mathurin Régnier, the libertine Saint-Amant, and generally throughout the poetic production of the period.[2]

SUCH SENTIMENTS are spun out at much greater length among prose writers of the late sixteenth and early seventeenth centuries. Montaigne's *Essais,* for example, include such titles as "De l'incertitude de nostre jugement" ["On the uncertainty of our judgment"—I, 47], or "Des vaines subtilitez" ["On vain subtleties"—I, 54], or "Comment nostre esprit s'empesche soy-mesme" ["How our mind confounds itself" —II,14], among others in the same vein. Montaigne's celebrated *Apologie de Raymond Sebond* offers, of course, a long critique of all forms of human knowledge. And in his last essay, Montaigne writes, in terms suggestive of Desportes or Malherbe, that the human mind

> ne faict que fureter et quester, et va sans cesse tournoiant, bastis-sant et s'empestrant en sa besongne.... Il pense remarquer de loing je ne sçay quelle apparence de clarté imaginaire; mais, pendant qu'il y court, tant de difficultez luy traversent la voye, d'empesche-mens et de nouvelles questes, qu'elles s'esgarent et l'enyvrent.

> [only searches and seeks, and goes incessantly turning about, building, and tripping over its creations.... It thinks it sees afar off who knows what appearance of imaginary clarity, but, as it runs toward it, so many difficulties cross its path, as much new quests as obstacles, that they lead it astray and befuddle it].[3]

The passage quoted above is among those closely followed by Montaigne's sometime disciple Pierre Charron, who reproduces almost textually Montaigne's thought on this subject. Charron believes, moreover, that the human mind is "un fonds d'obscurité plein de creux et de cachots, un labyrinthe, un abysme confus et bien entortillé ... " ["a pit of obscurity full of hollows and dungeons, a labyrinth, a gulf, confused and twisted ... "], among a great many similar passages.[4]

Possibly to the displeasure of Michel Foucault, both Montaigne and Charron seem explicitly to deny the notion of "real" links between word and thing, between language and its object, as attributed by Foucault to sixteenth-century thinkers. Thus Montaigne writes emphatically: "Il y a le nom et la chose: le nom, c'est une voix qui remerque et signifie la chose; le nom, ce n'est pas une partie de la chose ny de la

substance, c'est une piece estrangere joincte à la chose, et hors d'elle"
["There is the name and there is the thing: the name is a voice which
designates and means the thing; the name is not a part of the thing nor
of its substance, it is an extraneous part joined to the thing and outside
of it"]. Similarly, Charron writes that "le nom n'est rien de la nature et
substance de la chose, c'est seulement son image qui la représente, sa
marque qui la confronte et separe des autres" ["the name has nothing to
do with the nature and substance of the thing; it is only its image which
represents it, its mark which confronts it with and separates it from
other things"].[5]

One might wonder—and rightly so—what a Foucaldian thinker
might wish to make of Montaigne's and Charron's perceived need to
refute any "realist" theory of language. In any case, Foucault might also
view with displeasure—or see as left-handed confirmation—Montaigne's
and Charron's critique of reason, difference, and something very like
the Foucaldian *épistémè* of resemblance. In "De l'expérience," Montaigne
writes firmly, as part of a long critique of all the wretched, unrewarding
forms of thought:

> Il n'est desir plus naturel que le desir de connoissance. Nous
> essayons tous les moyens qui nous y peuvent mener. Quand la
> raison nous faut, nous y employons l'experience ... qui est un
> moyen plus foible et moins digne; mais la verité est chose si grande,
> que nous ne devons desdaigner aucune entremise qui nous y
> conduise. La raison a tant de formes, que nous ne sçavons à laquelle
> nous prendre; l'experience n'en a pas moins. La consequence que
> nous voulons tirer de la ressemblance des evenemens est mal seure,
> d'autant qu'ils sont tousjours dissemblables: il n'est aucune qualité
> si universelle en cette image des choses que la diversité et varieté....
> La ressemblance ne faict pas tant un comme la difference faict autre.

> [There is no desire more natural than the desire for knowledge. We
> try every means which may lead us to it. When reason fails, we use
> experience ... which is a weaker and less worthy method; but
> truth is so great a thing that we should not neglect any means of
> going toward it. Reason has so many forms, that we do not know
> which one to choose; experience has no fewer. The consequences
> we try to draw from the resemblance of events are risky, all the
> more so since they are always different; nothing is so universal in
> this image of things as diversity and variety.... Resemblance does
> not so much unify as difference dis-unites].[6]

In yet another passage closely imitated from Montaigne, Charron similarly criticizes reason, difference, and resemblances—but with a subtle difference. As part of a long critique of all forms of thought, a critique much like Montaigne's, Charron writes:

> C'est chose estrange, l'homme desire naturellement sçavoir la verité, et pour y parvenir, remue toutes choses, neantmoins il n'y peust parvenir. . . . L'homme est fort à desirer, et foible à prendre et tenir. Les deux principaux moyens qu'il employe pour parvenir à la cognoissance de la verité, sont la raison et l'experience. Or, tous deux sont si foibles et incertains (bien que l'experience plus), que n'en pouvons rien tirer de certain. La raison a tant de formes, est tant ployable, ondoyante, comme a esté dict en son lieu. L'experience encores plus, les evenements sont tousjours dissemblables: il n'y a rien si universel en la nature que la diversité, rien si rare et difficile et quasi impossible que la semblance. Et si l'on ne peust remarquer la dissemblance, c'est ignorance et foiblesse; ce qui s'entend de parfaicte, pur et entiere semblance et dissemblance: car, a vray dire, tous les deux sont par-tout: il n'y a aucune chose qui soit entierement semblable et dissemblable à une autre. C'est un ingenieux et merveilleux meslange et destrempement de nature. . . .

> [It is a strange thing: man naturally wants to know the truth and moves heaven and earth to gain it, but nevertheless cannot attain his goal. . . . Man is quick to desire, but poor at taking and holding. The two principal means he employs to attain knowledge of the truth are reason and experience. Now both of these are so weak and uncertain (although experience the more so), that we can derive nothing certain from them. Reason has so many forms and is so flexible and undulating, as has been said in its place. Experience is even more so, for events are always different: nothing is so universal in nature as diversity, nothing so rare and difficult and almost impossible as resemblance. And if one cannot see the differences, it is because of ignorance and weakness. For, to tell the truth, both are everywhere. There is nothing that is entirely similar or dissimilar to any other. Nature is an ingenious alloy and mixture. . .].[7]

In the passages quoted above, Montaigne regularly displays more equanimity, Charron more moral indignation. Where Montaigne is more eclectic, unwilling to disdain entirely any means at all which may lead to truth, Charron is more categorical. At the same time, however, Charron is more given to relativism. Although he continues to give difference priority over resemblance, he specifies that he means perfect and complete resemblance. For in Charron's world, as in Montaigne's, less-perfect resemblances abound.

Both Montaigne and Charron are considerably closer to Foucault's model of the *épistémè* of resemblance when they discuss in general terms the role of what might be called poetic intuition of the order of the world. For Montaigne, such intuition is a very important faculty indeed, since it links man with the harmony of nature and with that perfect knowledge which is known to God. Thus Montaigne writes, in the *Apologie de Raymond Sebond*, dating apparently from the late 1570s, that it would be unbelievable if "toute cette machine [the world] n'ait quelques marques empreintes de la main de ce grand architecte, et qu'il y ait quelque image és choses du monde, raportant aucunement à l'ouvrier qui les a basties et formées" ["this whole machine of the world did not bear some marks printed by the hand of this great architect, and that there were not some image in the things of this world linked to the worker who built and formed them"].[8]

Having evoked something like the Sartrean God the maker, the existing—or not-existing—fabricator of the world, Montaigne continues with a passage suggesting rather the *correspondances* of Baudelaire. Writing principally, apparently, in the 1580s and apparently following Plutarch, Montaigne declares:

> C'est ce qu'il nous dit luy mesme, que ses operations invisibles, il nous les manifeste par les visibles. . . . (*b*) Car ce monde est un temple tressainct, dedans lequel l'homme est introduict pour y contempler des statues, non ouvrées de mortelle main, mais celles que la divine pensée a faict sensibles: le Soleil, les estoiles, les eaux et la terre, pour nous representer les intelligibles.
>
> [This is what he tells us himself, that his invisible operations are manifested to us by visible ones. . . . (*b*) For this world is a most holy temple, in which man has been placed for the contemplation of statues not made by mortal hands, but rather those which the Divine thought has made perceptible: the sun, the stars, and the waters and the earth, to represent intelligible things.]

So lofty a view of divine semiology leads Montaigne to alter what a modern mind might take to be the normal order of priority between poetry and philosophy. Elsewhere in the *Apologie*, Montaigne asks a pointed rhetorical question:

Ay-je pas veu en Platon ce divin mot, que nature n'est rien qu'une poësie oenigmatique? comme peut estre qui diroit une peinture voilée et tenebreuse, entreluisant d'une infinie varieté de faux jours à exercer nos conjectures. . . . Et certes la philosophie n'est qu'une poësie sophistiquée. D'où tirent ces auteurs anciens toutes leurs authoritez, que des poëtes? Et les premiers furent poëtes eux mesmes et la traicterent en leur art.

[Have I not seen in Plato the divine aphorism that nature is nothing but an enigmatic poetry? Or as you might say, a veiled and murky painting, shining with an infinity of false lights to exercise our conjecture. . . . And indeed philosophy is nothing but a poetry for sophists. Where do these ancient authors get all their authorities but in the poets? And the first ones were poets themselves, and treated these subjects according to their art.]

Thus for Montaigne, who echoes here a commonplace of Renaissance thought, if philosophy is uncertain and even poetry may be enigmatic, nevertheless poetry has a clear superiority over philosophy, since it stands closer to the divine wisdom of God. Whereas a modern reader might suppose that philosophers are somehow more logical, more serious-minded and reasonable than poets, Montaigne places even so sublime a thinker as Plato in an inferior relationship to poetry on this score. For Montaigne, in a striking concluding sentence to the last passage quoted above, "Platon n'est qu'un poëte descousu" ["Plato is nothing but a poet who is incoherent"].[9]

In these passages at least, following more or less faithfully certain ancient and Renaissance sources, Montaigne expresses remarkable respect for poetic knowledge, in which indeed he seems to see something like the Foucaldian *épistémè* of resemblance, both in the strength of poetic intuition and divine signs and in the enigmatic quality of these signs in nature. His views are largely shared, moreover, by Charron—but again with certain subtle differences.

For Charron, poetry and philosophy stand on something like an equal footing. "La philosophie," he writes, "semble suader gratieusement et vouloir plaire en profitant, comme la poësie" ["Philosophy . . . seems to graciously persuade and tries to please while edifying, like poetry"]. And thus the sage must be ready to use both as he "produit et fait marcher en belle ordonnance, sentences, et aphorismes de la philosophie, similitudes, exemples, histoires, beaux mots triés de toutes les mines et thresors vieux et nouveaux . . . " ["produces and trots out in proper order proverbs and aphorisms of philosophy, comparisons, examples, stories, and witty sayings selected from all the mines and treasures, old and new . . . "]. Charron compares favorably the relatively more poetic Socrates with the relatively more legalistic Aristotle. Nevertheless — and even though he himself occasionally waxes poetic in the pursuit of wisdom — Charron finally places poetry in the domain of "imagination." In this category, according to Charron, properly belong "les inventions, les faceties et brocards, les pointes et subtilitéz, les fictions et mensonges, les figures et comparaisons, la proprieté, netteté, elegance, gentillesse. Parquoy appartiennent à elle la poësie, l'Eloquence, Musique, et generalement tout ce qui consiste en figure, correspondance, harmonie et proportion" ["inventions, jokes, broad humor, fictions and lies, figures and comparisons, propriety, clarity, elegance, and gentleness. For which reason poetry also belongs to it, as well as eloquence, music, and in general everything that consists of figures, correspondences, harmonies, and proportion"].[10]

But if both writers accord importance to the notion of poetic intuition, both writers also accord importance to the equally Foucaldian notion of representation and classification. Although both wrote some years before any abrupt shift, as posited by Foucault, from an *épistémè* of resemblance to an *épistémè* of representation, neither one is a stranger to notions of classification, generalization, regularization, and the like. Montaigne, of course, is celebrated for taking all sides of a question. And, possibly in contradiction with texts of his quoted above, Montaigne writes elsewhere that "La sagesse est un bastiment solide et entier, dont chaque piece tient son rang et porte sa marque . . ." ["Wisdom is a solid and complete building, in which each piece has its rank and carries its mark. . . "]. In another passage, however, he doubts — perhaps more characteristically — whether that comprehensive structure of knowledge can be adequately described. In the absence of evident general principles, he writes:

> Je laisse aux artistes, et ne sçay s'ils en viennent à bout en chose si meslée, si menue et fortuite, de renger en bandes cette infinie diversité de visages et arrester nostre inconstance et la mettre par ordre. Non seulement je trouve malaisé d'attacher nos actions les unes aux autres, mais chacune à part soy je trouve mal-aysé de la designer proprement par quelque qualité principalle, tant elles sont doubles et bigarrées à divers lustres.

[I leave it to the artists, and I don't know if even they can master something so mixed up, so minuscule and fortuitous, to arrange in classes that infinite diversity of faces and stop our inconstancy and put it all in order. Not only do I find it difficult to attach our actions to one another, but each one separately I find difficult to label by some salient, principal quality, so much are they doubled and mixed with diverse aspects].[11]

For his part, Charron not only echoes Montaigne's pessimism but also displays greater confidence in understanding arrived at through identification of salient factors and relative proportions—that is, an *épistémè* of classification and representation. Thus, despite some Montaigne-like vacillation elsewhere, Charron writes in one place that one cannot hope to live well "si premierement on ne sçait en quel rang l'on doibt tenir les choses, les richesses, la santé, la beauté, la noblesse, la science, etc., et leurs contraires" ["if first one does not know what rank to assign to things, riches, health, beauty, nobility, knowledge, etc., and their opposites"]. Charron adds, with presumably characteristic ambiguity, that "C'est une haute et belle science que de la presseance et preeminence des choses: mais bien difficile . . . " ["It is a high and beautiful science, to study the precedence and pre-eminence of things, although very difficult . . . "]. And he adds—just as La Rochefoucauld was to write some sixty years later—that "il faut apprendre à bien justement estimer les choses, et leur donner le prix et le rang, qui leur appartiennent, qui est le vray faict de prudence et suffisance. C'est un haut point de philosophie . . . " ["One must learn to estimate things very correctly and give them the price and the rank which belong to them, such is the true nature of prudence and adequacy. It is a high point of philosophy . . . "].[12]

THUS IT MAY well be, as critical commentary suggests, that Charron's view represents a subtle evolution with respect to Montaigne's—that Charron's moral bias, among other factors, may have led him somewhat further from poetic intuition and closer to practical relativism, pragmatic epistemology, and empirical rule-making more characteristic of a later age. It may well be then, as Renée Kögel writes in a recent commentary, that Charron "has great confidence that he can prescribe rules" for a relatively mathematized understanding of the world—all as part of Charron's conviction that "l'art et l'invention semblent non seulement imiter nature, mais la passer . . . " ["art and invention not only seem to imitate nature, they surpass it . . . "].[13]

At the same time, however, with respect to the epistemological issues presented above, Montaigne and Charron are far less different from each other than from later thinkers, such as Descartes. When viewed in this latter perspective, Montaigne's and Charron's critiques of all forms of knowledge stand in sharp contrast to Descartes's willingness—or eagerness—to overlook or pare away difficulty. And Montaigne's and Charron's diffuse, convoluted style, an appropriate expression of their epistemological approach, stands in truly striking contrast with Descartes's limpid prose.

Thus in his *Regulae,* apparently written about 1628, Descartes asserts that "il ne faut s'occuper que des objets dont notre esprit paraît capable d'acquerir une connaissance certaine et indubitable" [recent French translation of the Latin original—"we must not concern ourselves with anything except those things about which our mind can acquire certain and indubitable knowledge"]. Elsewhere in the *Regulae,* Descartes writes:

Nous sommes avertis...qu'il ne faut mêler absolument aucune conjecture aux jugements que nous portons sur la vérité des choses....car la vraie raison pour laquelle on n'a jamais rien trouvé dans la philosophie habituelle d'assez évident et d'assez certain pour pouvoir être soustrait à la controverse, c'est d'abord que les hommes d'étude, non contents de connaître des choses claires et certaines, ont osé affirmer aussi des choses obscures et inconnues, auxquelles ils n'arrivaient que par des conjectures probables, et qu'ensuite, y ajoutant eux-mêmes peu à peu une foi entière et les mêlant indistinctement aux choses vraies et évidentes, ils ont fini par ne pouvoir rien conclure qui ne parût dépendre de quelque proposition de cette sorte et qui par suite ne fût incertain.

[We are aware that we must mix absolutely no conjecture into the judgments we make about the truth of things. . . . because the real reason why ordinary philosophy has never found anything evident and certain enough to be free of all controversy is, first, that studious men, not content with knowing clear and certain things, have dared to allege also things that are obscure and unknown, to which they accede only by probable conjectures, and to which, subsequently they little by little add full faith and mix them indistinguishably with the true and evident things, in the end they can conclude nothing which does not appear to depend on some proposition of that kind and which, in consequence, appears uncertain.][14]

Descartes explains further that, if one is to achieve the hoped-for result, the intellectual options are limited: "Pour ne pas tomber ensuite dans la même erreur, nous allons énumérer ici tous les actes de notre entendement, par lesquels nous pouvons parvenir à la connaissance des choses sans aucune crainte d'erreur; il n'y en a que deux: l'intuition et la déduction" ["In order not to fall into the same error, we will now enumerate all the acts of our understanding through which we can attain knowledge of things without any fear of error; there are only two of these: intuition and deduction"].[15]

Descartes, therefore, does not entirely abandon the notion of intuition. He shows it not only still operating to achieve direct and ultimately correct knowledge of the world but also redefines its method and its object. He writes:

> Par *intuition* j'entends, non pas le témoignage changeant des sens ou le jugement trompeur d'une imagination qui compose mal son objet, mais la conception d'un esprit pur et attentif, conception si facile et si distincte qu'aucun doute ne reste sur ce que nous comprenons. . . . Ainsi chacun peut voir par intuition qu'il existe, qu'il pense, que le triangle est défini par trois lignes seulement, la sphère par une seule surface, et des choses de ce genre, qui sont bien plus nombreuses que ne le pourraient croire la plupart des hommes, parce qu'ils dédaignent de tourner leur esprit vers des choses si faciles.

> [By *intuition* I mean, not the changing evidence of the senses or the illusory judgment of an imagination which poorly conceives its object, but the conception of a pure and attentive mind, a conception so easy and so distinct that no doubt remains about what we understand. . . . Thus anyone can see by intuition that he exists, that he thinks, that the triangle is defined by three lines only, the sphere by a single surface, and things of this type, which are much more numerous than most men believe, because they disdain to turn their mind toward such easy things].[16]

Thus for Descartes, certainty is the only mental standard worthy of a philosopher. The ways to attain it, intuition and reason, are limited; but the number of certainties attainable is large. In this passage at least, something like an early version of the Cartesian "interior light" conquers all. So much so, indeed, that for Descartes the only true criterion of truth or valid philosophical activity may be simple facility—the possibly aristocratic, Castiglione-like ease with which truth may be discovered.

Whereas Montaigne asserts that "de aucune chose [l]es hommes, je dy les sçavans les mieux nais, les plus suffisans, ne sont d'accord, non pas que le ciel soit sur nostre teste . . ." ["of no thing are men, and I mean the wisest and the most high born, the most accomplished, in agreement, not even that the sky is above our heads . . ."], Descartes graciously explains what has led wise men astray. Whereas Montaigne laments "le trouble que nostre jugement nous donne à nous mesmes, et l'incertitude que chacun sent en soy . . ." ["the distress that our judgment gives us, and the uncertainty that everyone feels in himself . . ."], Descartes speaks imperturbably of the infallible conceptions of a pure and attentive mind.[17]

With respect to their critique of knowledge and their convoluted intellectual style, Montaigne and Charron differ relatively little. Concerning themselves, like the poets Desportes and Malherbe, with some baroque image of the thought process, Montaigne and Charron may well represent something like a Kuhnian crisis-state in intellectual history. By the same token Cartesian clarity may well represent something like a Kuhnian new paradigm of knowledge, nourished by a different style, a different set of objects, and a different description of the intellectual process. Any posited "Cartesian" revolution in intellectual history thus may appear also as a Kuhnian scientific revolution, perhaps as movement from one Foucaldian épistémè to another. At the same time, however, none of the texts quoted above is a perfect expression of any of these doctrines. Each one contains elements contradictory to a Kuhnian and, especially, a Foucaldian description of the movement of thought. All the transformations suggested above point to movement of a specifically epistemological nature. Yet each one participates in the irregularity and particularity of structure suggested by Deleuze—or even, at the limit, by the more skeptical Feyerabend or the eternal essentialists. No text perfectly fits the modern criteria. Comparison of texts as wholes, however, shows clearly that something has changed. The rate of change, moreover, has been unequal. Montaigne and Charron are more similar than either is to Descartes. Descartes and La Rochefoucauld (or Charron and La Rochefoucauld) are more similar than either is to Montaigne. Something is unusually different in underlying epistemological assumptions and style. And, in one way or another, that difference will be worked out and applied in a variety of texts throughout the seventeenth century.

NOTES

1. Desportes, *Diverses amours* (Geneva: Droz, 1963), pp. 21, 44, 70, 100, 131–32, 188, 197; *Diane,* 1 (Geneva: Droz, 1959), pp. 40, 41, 125, 146; *Amours d'Hippolyte* (Geneva: Droz, 1960), pp. 15, 106, 124. See also *Diverses amours,* pp. 161, 184, and *Diane,* 1: 34, 81, 82, 92–93, 161, 183, 187, etc. Dates of first publication, 1573–87.

2. Malherbe, *Oeuvres poétiques* (Paris: Les Belles Lettres, 1968) 1: 122, 126, 174, 178, 245. See also pp. 29, 43, 221. The poet Francis Ponge finds it striking that, thirty or forty years before Descartes, Malherbe writes lines like: "Qu'en dis-tu, ma raison? crois-tu qu'il soit possible/D'avoir du jugement, et ne l'adorer pas?" (*Pour un Malherbe* [Paris: Gallimard, 1965], p. 16).

3. Montaigne, *Essais* (Paris: Pléiade, 1950), p. 1198.

4. Charron, *De la sagesse* (Paris, 1789), 1: 165, 176, 183.

5. Montaigne, *Essais,* p. 697; Charron, *Sagesse* (Paris, 1607), p. 297 (I: 60); quoted in R. Kögel, *Pierre Charron* (Geneva: Droz, 1972), p. 115, with an apparently incorrect reference.

6. Montaigne, *Essais,* pp. 1194–95.

7. Charron, *Sagesse* (1789), pp. 36–38.

8. Montaigne, *Essais,* p. 491.

9. Ibid., pp. 491, 600–601.

10. Charron, *Sagesse* (Paris, 1604), pp. 6, 75, 85.

11. Montaigne, *Essais,* p. 1209.

12. Charron, *Sagesse* (1789), pp. 536, 538–39.

13. Kögel, *Charron.* p. 35; Charron, *Sagesse* (1789), p. 179.

14. Descartes, *Oeuvres et lettres* (Paris: Pléiade, 1953), pp. 43–44. The Pléiade edition offers this modern French translation of Descartes's original Latin, thought to have been composed about 1628. For other discussion of Foucault and Descartes, see Sylvie Romanowski, *L'Illusion chez Descartes. La Structure du discours cartésien* (Paris: Klincksieck, 1974).

15. Descartes, *Oeuvres.*

16. Ibid.

17. Montaigne, *Essais,* p. 633.

CHAPTER 4

Two Modes of Thought in *L'Astrée*

HONORÉ D'URFÉ'S long and long-celebrated seventeenth-century pastoral novel *L'Astrée* presents a clear epistemological dimension and a familiar image of the thought process. In *L'Astrée,* as in a great many texts presented previously, "l'esprit vole incessamment d'un penser en un autre . . . " ["the mind flies incessantly from one thought to another . . . "]. The heroine Astrée wanders in a "labyrinthe de diverses pensées" ["labyrinth of divers thoughts"]. And the hero Céladon walks by a river's edge striking the water "du bout de sa houlette, dont il ne touchoit point tant de gouttes d'eau, que de divers pensers le venoient assaillir, qui flottants comme l'onde, n'estoient point si tost arrivez, qu'ils en estoient chassez par d'autres plus violents" ["with the end of his crook, with which he didn't touch so many drops of water as there were divers thoughts which came to assail him, which thoughts, floating like the wave, had no sooner arrived than they were chased away by other, more violent ones"]. In one of the poetic pieces interspersed with his prose narrative, Honoré d'Urfé describes in paradoxical terms the knowledge derived from experience:

> L'experience n'est que d'avoir espreuvé
> Cent diverses humeurs, et s'estre conservé.
> Ce qui nous rend prudens, c'est doncques l'inconstance.

> [Experience is nothing but having felt a hundred divers humors and to have stayed alive. Thus, that which makes us prudent is inconstance].

In *L'Astrée* the shepherdess Diane, like Montaigne and Charron, criticizes knowledge derived from opinion, heaping reproaches on the shepherdess Philis because "l'opinion a plus de puissance sur vous que la verité, et . . . c'est par elle que vous êtes conduite" ["opinion has more power over you than truth, and it is by the former that you are led"]. The shepherd Silvandre explains to the nymph Léonide that, as indeed everyone in the world of *L'Astrée* already knows, "les troubles mouvements des sens empeschent infiniment la clarté de l'entendement, et comme aux contre-pois d'une orloge l'un ne peut monter que l'autre ne descende, aussi, quand les sens s'eslevent, l'entendement s'abaisse" ["the troubled movements of the senses infinitely hinder clarity of understanding, and just as one counterweight of a clock cannot rise without the other descending, also, when the senses rise, understanding fades"].[1]

Like the poets of the late sixteenth and early seventeenth centuries, Silvandre also believes that "Ce qui attire quelque chose ... doit avoir quelque sympathie avec elle" ["What attracts something should have some sympathy with it"] (1: 240). In general, in *L'Astrée*, "toutes les choses corporelles ou spirituelles ont chacune leurs contraires, et leurs sympathisantes; des plus petites nous pourrions venir à la preuve des plus grandes" ["all things corporal and spiritual have their respective opposites and their sympathies; from the smallest we can come to proof of the greatest"] (1: 167). The world of sympathies and antipathies lives harmoniously with the natural order, and, as one personage observes in a later volume, the gods "n'assemblent jamais les contraires sans quelque lieu de sympathie ... " ["never join contraries without some link of sympathy ... "] (3: 422).

Although *L'Astrée* is a pastoral novel whose scene is reduced to the tiny province of Forez and whose action concerns principally the life of shepherds and shepherdesses, the novel's world is actually a kind of microcosm including bits and pieces of a great deal more. Despite the pastoral personages' propensity for the simple life, their world has room for a possibly baroque assortment of queens and princesses, of nymphs and knights in armor, of city dwellers and Druidic priests and soothsayers. The borders of the province are open, and passing travelers tell stories of distant places. Life is long in the peaceful province, moreover, and nymphs and shepherds have lived other lives under different circumstances. Some have traveled or been educated outside the province and have spoken with people well informed on late imperial Roman politics, Druidic theology, or life in early London or among the Visigoths, all of which subjects find their way into the repertoire of allegedly mannerist *meriviglie* — or baroque organic unity and metamorphosis, or indeed pre-precious ornamentation — in d'Urfé's text.

Perhaps most striking of all, although the intellectual alternatives available to shepherds living in a far-off province in the fifth century A.D. might in reality reasonably be limited to Christian and pagan religious beliefs, perhaps mixed with superstition and Platonic or other classical philosophy, in point of fact *L'Astrée* also owes something to new science and new invention as understood in early seventeenth-century France. One recurring personage in the novel is the unscrupulous Climante, a kind of amateur scientist who uses bizarre, Rube Goldberg–like machinery to further his evil schemes. In volume one the nymph Léonide, lodged fortuitously in a country inn, overhears Climante describe in detail the scientific trick he used to deceive Léonide and some of her friends when they recently visited his false soothsayer's temple. Climante explains:

> Au devant du miroir, il y avait une aiz, sur laquelle Hecate estoit peinte: ceste aiz avoit tout le bas ferré d'un fusil, et comme vous sçavez, elle ne tenoit qu'à quelques poils de cheval, si deliez, qu'avec l'obscurité du lieu, il n'y avoit personne qui les peust appercevoir; aussi tost que l'on les tiroit, l'aiz tomboit, et de sa pesanteur frappoit du fusil sur une pierre si à propos, qu'elle ne manquoit presque jamais de faire feu. J'avois mis au mesme lieu une mixtion de soulphre, et de salpestre, qui s'esprend de sorte au feu qui le touche, qu'il s'en esleve une flamme, avec une si grande promptitude, qu'il n'y a celuy qui n'en demeure en quelque sorte estonné: ce que j'avois inventé pour faire croire que c'estoit une espece, ou de divinité, ou d'enchantement. . . .

> [In front of the mirror, there was a plank on which Hecate was painted. This plank had the whole lower end sheathed in steel, and, as you know, it was suspended only by a few horsehairs, so fine that in the half darkness of the place no one could possibly notice them. When one pulled them away, the plank fell, and with all its weight struck a stone hard enough so that it almost never failed to strike a spark. At that same spot I had placed a mixture of sulphur and saltpeter that caught in such a way when sparks touched it, that a flame suddenly billowed up, and scarcely anyone could help but be dumbfounded—all of which I had invented to make people believe it was some kind of divinity or magic . . .](1: 158).

Climante returns with similar magic tricks in subsequent volumes (e.g., 4: 28–29), in every case opposing the doubtful magic of scientific knowledge to the true magic of the high priest Adamas, the Druids, and their friends.

Just as Druidic mysticism curiously coexists with do-it-yourself science in the novel, the thoughts and deliberations of Honoré d'Urfé's personages are based on a variety of intellectual styles and assumptions.

Indeed, in debating moral, scientific, and religious questions, the shepherds, shepherdesses, Druids, nymphs, and princes use at least two sharply contrasting means of arriving at their various conclusions. The problems posed by these heterogeneous epistemological approaches profoundly affect the worldview of the novel. At the same time they are suggestive with respect to the movement of intellect in seventeenth-century France.

THE CONTRASTS in *L'Astrée* can perhaps be best illustrated by two texts, appearing in the first and second volumes of the novel respectively. The first text is one of the pastoral work's numerous shepherds' debates—in this case between the notoriously inconstant lover, Hylas, and the constant or nearly Platonically "perfect" lover, Tyrcis. As might perhaps be expected, their half-humorous discussion concerns primarily the merits of their respective approaches:

> Et à quoy cognoissez vous, respondit Hylas, que je n'aime point?—Je le cognois, dit Tyrcis, à vostre perpetuel changement.—Nous sommes, dit-il, d'une bien differente opinion, car j'ay tousjours creu que l'ouvrier se rendoit plus parfait, plus il exerçoit souvent le mestier dont il faisoit profession.—Cela est vray, respondit Tyrcis, quand on suit les regles de l'art, mais quand on fait autrement, il advient comme à ceux qui s'estant fourvoyez, plus ils marchent, et plus ils s'esloignent de leur chemin. Et c'est pourquoy, tout ainsi que la pierre qui roule continuellement, ne se revestit jamais de mousse, mais plustost d'ordure et de salleté, de mesme vostre legereté se peut bien acquerir de la honte, mais non jamais de l'amour. Il faut que vous sçachiez, Hylas, que les blessures d'Amour sont de telle qualité, que jamais elles ne guerissent.—Dieu me garde, dit Hylas, d'un tel blesseur.—Vous avez raison, repliqua Tyrcis, car si à chaque fois que vous avez esté blessé d'une nouvelle beauté, vous aviez receu une playe incurable, je ne sçay si en tout vostre corps il y auroit plus une place saine, mais aussi vous estes privé de ces douceurs et de ces felicitez, qu'Amour donne aux vrais amants, et cela miraculeusement (comme toutes ses autres actions) par la mesme blessure qu'il leur a faite. Que si la langue pouvoit bien exprimer ce que le coeur ne peut entierement gouster, et qu'il vous fust permis d'ouyr les secrets de ce dieu, je ne croy pas que vous ne voulussiez renoncer à vostre infidelité.

["And how do you know," answered Hylas, "that I am not in love?"

"I know it," said Tyrcis, "by your never-ending changes of heart."

"We are," he said, "of very different opinions, for I have always believed that any worker perfected his skill, the more often he exercised his profession."

"That's true," answered Tyrcis, "when you follow the rules of the art, but when one does otherwise, he is more like those who, when they take a wrong turn, go farther from the path the longer they walk. And that is why, just like a rolling stone that never gathers moss but only filth and dirt, your frivolity may gain you shame, but never love. You must know, Hylas, that the wounds of love are such that they can never be cured."

"God save me," said Hylas, "from such wounds as those."

"You're right," replied Tyrcis. "For if every time you were wounded by a new beauty, you had received an incurable wound, I don't know if there would be a single healthy spot anywhere on your body. But also, you're deprived of those pleasures and happiness that love gives to true lovers—and gives miraculously (as in all his other actions) by the very wound he makes. So that if the tongue could well express what the heart cannot wholly feel, and if you were permitted to hear the secrets of this god, I doubt you would hesitate to renounce your infidelity."] (1: 28–29).

Hylas's and Tyrcis's debate was first published in 1607. The remarkably different second text appears in *L'Astrée*'s second volume, first published in 1610. In it the nymph Léonide gives her verdict on a lovers' quarrel presented to her and her fellow nymphs for judgment. After the three principals have told the rather complicated story of their relationships, she is asked to decide whether the shepherdess Célidée should prefer the young Calidon or her older suitor Thamire:

JUGEMENT DE LA NYMPHE LEONIDE

Trois choses se presentent à nos yeux sur le differend de Celidée, Thamire et Calidon: la premiere, l'amour; la deuxiesme, le devoir; et la derniere, l'offense. En la premiere, nous remarquons trois grandes affections; en la deuxiesme, trois grandes obligations; et en la derniere, trois grandes injures. Celidée dés le berceau a aimé Thamire, Thamire a aimé Celidée estant des-ja avancé en aage, et Calidon l'a aimée dés sa jeunesse. Celidée a esté obligée à la vertueuse affection de Thamire, Thamire l'a esté à la memoire du pere de Calidon, et Calidon aux bons offices de Thamire. Et en fin Celidée a esté fort offensée de Thamire quand il l'a voulu remettre à Calidon, et Calidon n'a pas moins offensé Thamire et Celidée: Thamire, en luy refusant la mesme courtoisie qu'il avoit receue de luy, et Celidée, en la recherchant contre sa volonté, et luy faisant perdre celuy qu'elle aimoit.

Toutes ces choses longuement debattues et bien considerées, nous avons cogneu que, tout ainsi que les choses que nature produict, sont toujours plus parfaictes que celles qui procedent de l'art, de mesme l'amour qui vient par inclination, est plus grande et plus estimable que celle qui procede du dessein ou de l'obligation. Davantage, les obligations que nous recevons en nostre personne mesme, estans plus grandes que celles que la consideration d'autruy nous represente, il est certain qu'un bien-faict oblige plus que ceste memoire. Et en fin si l'offense meslée avec l'ingratitude est plus griefve que celle qui seulement nous offense, il n'y a personne qui n'advoue celuy-là estre plus punissable, qui les commet toutes deux. Or nous cognoissons que l'amour de Thamire procede d'inclination, puis qu'ordinairement celles qui sont telles, sont reciproques, et qu'aussi aimant Celidée, il en a esté aymé, ce qui n'est pas advenu à Calidon, de qui l'infertile affection n'a rien produict que de la peine et du mespris. . . .

C'est pourquoy, en premier lieu, nous ordonnons que l'amour de Calidon cede à l'amour de Thamire, que l'obligation de Thamire soit estimée moindre que celle de Calidon, et l'offense de Calidon plus grande que celle de Thamire. Et quant à ce qui concerne Thamire et Celidée, nous déclarons que Celidée a plus d'obligation à Thamire, mais que Thamire l'a plus offensée, d'autant qu'il l'a aymée avec tant d'honnesteté, et eslevée avec tant de soing, qu'elle seroit ingratte, si elle ne s'en tenoit obligée. Mais l'offence qu'il luy a faicte n'a pas esté petite, lors qu'au desavantage de son affection, il a voulu satisfaire aux obligations qu'il pensoit avoir à Calidon. Et toutesfois, d'autant qu'il n'y a offense qui ne soit vaincue par la personne qui ayme bien, nous ordonnons, de l'advis de tous ceux qui ont ouy avec nous ce different, que l'amour de Celidée surmontera l'offense qu'elle a receue de Thamire, et que l'amour que Thamire luy portera à l'advenir surpassera en eschange celle que luy a portée Celidée jusques icy: Car tel est nostre jugement.

[JUDGMENT OF THE NYMPH LEONIDE

Three things are before us concerning the quarrel of Célidée, Thamire, and Calidon: first, love; second, duty; and last, offenses. In the first, we take note of three great affections; in the second, three great obligations; and in the last, three great injuries. From the cradle, Célidée has loved Thamire; Thamire came to love Célidée when already advanced in age, and Calidon loved her from his youth. Célidée was obligated by the virtuous affection of Thamire, just as Thamire was to the memory of Calidon's father, and Calidon to the good offices of Thamire. And finally Célidée was greatly offended by Thamire when he tried to cede her to Calidon; Calidon did no less offense to Thamire and Célidée: to Thamire by refusing him the same courtesy he had received from him, and to Célidée, by pursuing her against her will, so that she lost the person she loved.

All these things debated at length and carefully considered, we have recognized that, just as the things which nature makes are more nearly perfect than those produced by art, so love that comes from inclination is greater and more admirable than that which comes from intention or obligation. Moreover, the obligations which we incur in our own person being greater than those we honor out of consideration for others, it is certain that a benefit creates a greater obligation than a remembrance. And finally if offense mixed with ingratitude is more grievous than that which merely offends us, no one will deny that he who commits both is more worthy of punishment. Now we know that Thamire's love proceeds from inclination, since ordinarily those that do are reciprocated, and that loving Célidée he was loved in return, which was not the case for Calidon, whose infertile affection produced nothing but pain and scorn....

This is why, in the first instance, we order that Calidon's love give way to that of Thamire, that Thamire's obligation be judged less than Calidon's, and Calidon's offense greater than Thamire's. And as regards Thamire and Célidée, we declare that Célidée is more obligated to Thamire, but that Thamire has more offended her, since he loved her so nobly and raised her so carefully, that she would be ungrateful if she did not recognize her obligation. But the offense he caused was no small one, since to the disadvantage of his own affection, he decided to satisfy his supposed obligations to Calidon. And yet, because there are no offenses which cannot be overcome by someone who loves deeply, we order, with the concurrence of all those who have heard this case with us, that the love of Célidée shall overcome the offense she has received from Thamire, and that the love Thamire shall bring her in the future shall surpass in exchange that which Célidée has shown him up to now. For such is our judgment.] (2: 72–73).

While these two texts display certain similarities, their most striking difference is no doubt in their respective approaches to the problems with which they attempt to deal. In the first text, having registered a difference of opinion with Tyrcis, Hylas draws an analogy between lovers who improve their technique through practice and workers who improve the more often they exercise their profession. Tyrcis responds with a second analogy: Those who practice incorrectly do not improve with time, because they are like those who, having once taken a wrong turn, get farther from their destination the longer they walk. The beginning of Tyrcis's next sentence, "And that is why," suggests a causal relationship between what precedes and what follows. In this case, however, what follows is a second analogy, a proverb as venerable in French as in English: a rolling stone gathers no moss. Extending the proverb's meaning, Tyrcis evokes a stone rolling "continuellement" and states that not only will it gather no moss, but will instead be covered with filth and dirt. At the same time he alters slightly the proverb's traditional significances: frivolity never gains love, only shame. A little farther on, Tyrcis and Hylas both play on the possible physical effects of the poetic "wounds of love." Hylas prefers not to be wounded; Tyrcis agrees he is right, since "si à chaque fois que vous avez esté blessé d'une nouvelle beauté, vous aviez receu une playe incurable, je ne sçay si en tout vostre corps il y auroit plus une place saine."

Thus both Hylas's and Tyrcis's style of debate proceeds from variations on proverbial and poetic analogies. Unsupported by any other kind of justification, their remarks must depend exclusively on whatever merit lies in the idea that inconstant lovers actually are like rolling stones, or that the wounds of love actually do hurt, or that even platonic lovers can hope, like apprentice artisans, to improve with practice. Both debaters, therefore, make use of specifically poetic wisdom, according to that same tradition considered superior to philosophy by Montaigne and admired by Ronsard.

At the same time, however, Hylas's and Tyrcis's debate implies certain difficulties and weaknesses of method. For if one essential statement to be made about lovers is that they resemble workers, lost people, or rolling stones, there may exist no general rule to prove that they are not also like sick people, the victims of tyrants, or persons with deep taproots planted in their hearts—all of which additional comparisons are adduced by Hylas and Tyrcis in the pages following the text quoted above. Under such a system, for reasons abundantly developed by Montaigne and Charron among others in the last decades of the sixteenth century, each metaphor must be examined on its merits. There may thus exist no general understanding of the extent to which one may be argued or extended, nor any general method of explaining the relationship between various analogies presented. Hylas and Tyrcis may thus possess no general method of discovering possible relationships between rolling stones and taproots, between workers and victims of tyrants, between the lost and the sick, other than what still further analogies may suggest. And this is true even though such comparisons are somehow associated with—and thus validated by—the miracles of the god of love.

FOR LÉONIDE, rendering judgment in volume two of *L'Astrée,* truth is something other than rolling stones or incurable wounds. Her judgment is fairly long, and as such it sacrifices much of the spontaneity and apparently direct, Dionysian wisdom of Hylas and Tyrcis. As Léonide herself remarks, she draws her conclusions only when "Toutes ces choses" have been "longuement debattues et bien considerées." At the same time, however, her longer discourse nevertheless resolves itself into the repetition of a rather simple schematic procedure—a kind of algorithm, embarked upon more confidently than any in Charron, of sentiment. Attempting to discover whether Célidée should love Calidon or Thamire, she immediately formulates the problem in terms of three fundamental criteria of analysis: "Trois choses se presentent à nos yeux," she declares, "la premiere, l'amour; la deuxiesme, le devoir; et la derniere, l'offense." To lovers who have loved as much as Hylas or waited in vain for solutions as long as Céladon, such a formulation might appear excessively formalistic or even simplistic. Montaigne's and Charron's view that universal difference and universal resemblance make meaningful categorization difficult or impossible is implicitly rejected. Attempting the accurate classification and evaluation of things recommended by Charron, but without any of the difficulty Charron feared in such a procedure, Léonide chooses not from any very extensive set of categories—nor indeed from any indefinitely extensible set of categories—but from a rather small, explicitly limited, symmetrical, and hence relatively Cartesian or representational system. Léonide next sees three significant examples of each category in the quarrel before her: "En la premiere, nous remarquons trois grandes affections; en la deuxiesme, trois grandes obligations; et en la derniere, trois grandes injures."

47

In her second paragraph Léonide enunciates principles permitting her and her hearers to arrange loves, obligations, and offenses on scales of value. She sees different loves not as ingenious mixtures of nature but as straightforward phenomena to be graded in essentially quantitative fashion. Her other statements of principle also imply quantitative differences between varying examples of obligation and offense. Thus she suggests that "les obligations que nous recevons en nostre personne mesme, estans plus grandes que celles que la consideration d'autruy nous represente, il est certain qu'un bien-faict oblige plus que ceste memoire." And that "si l'offense meslée avec l'ingratitude est plus griefve que celle qui seulement nous offense, il n'y a personne qui n'advoue celuy-là estre plus punissable, qui les commet toutes deux."

These and similar quantifying principles are applied to the examples in Léonide's second, third, and fourth paragraphs. She observes that "nous cognoissons que l'amour de Thamire procede d'inclination, puis qu'ordinairement celles qui sont telles, sont reciproques, et qu'aussi aimant Celidée, il en a esté aymé. . . . " And so on, until each of her three personages has been placed on a scale of value with respect to each category. Having dealt with the issues in this manner, Léonide is then ready to eliminate the lesser loves, duties, and injuries in favor of the greater. Like King Tulle in Corneille's *Horace,* she concludes that one obligation shall give way to another. Léonide saves the most difficult problem for the last part of her decision, until—as so many kings and others would do in the great Cornelian theater of the following decades —she ends her judgment with the command that one personage love another: "nous ordonnons . . . que l'amour de Celidée surmontera l'offense qu'elle a receue de Thamire, et que l'amour que Thamire luy portera à l'advenir surpassera en eschange celle que luy a portée Celidée jusques icy. . . . "

As may readily be deduced from the previous chapters, examples of such sublime confidence in schemes of classification as a means of resolving sentimental problems may be difficult to discover among French authors in the fifty years before publication of the second volume of *L'Astrée.* Léonide's approach, of course, has little to do with the irregularly organized essays of Montaigne, or the complex and indefinitely extensible hierarchies of the so-called great chain of being as understood in the Renaissance. It has much more to do, just as clearly, with the schematic style of Descartes's *Discours de la méthode,* first published twenty-seven years later. Léonide's method, like Descartes's, seeks to "ne comprendre rien de plus en mes jugements que ce qui se présenterait si clairement et si distinctement à mon esprit que je n'eusse aucune occasion de le mettre en doute" ["include nothing in my judgments that did not stand out so clearly and so distinctly to my mind that there was no reason to doubt it"]. She is resigned to certain arbitrary qualities in her categories, apparently believing like Descartes that "pour le commencement, il vaut mieux ne se servir que de celles qui se présentent d'elles-mêmes à nos sens, et que nous ne saurions ignorer . . . que d'en chercher de plus rares et étudiées . . . " ["in the beginning, it is better to use only those which present themselves spontaneously to our senses and which we cannot ignore . . . rather than to seek out rarer and more subtle ones . . . "]. Whereas Montaigne, Charron, Hylas, and Tyrcis encounter difficulty in identifying the relative importance of factors in concrete situations, Léonide is supremely confident in her ability to evaluate occurrences in terms of salient factors. Like Descartes, she believes it appropriate to "diviser chacune des difficultez que j'examinerais en autant de parcelles qu'il se pourroit. . . . [et] conduire par ordre mes pensées, en commençant par les objets les plus simples et les plus aisez à connaître, pour monter peu à peu, comme par degrés, jusques à la connaissance des plus composés; et supposant même de l'ordre entre ceux qui ne se précèdent point naturellement les uns les autres" ["divide each of the difficulties that I might examine in as many parts as possible. . . . (and) to conduct my thoughts in order, beginning with the simplest and easiest objects to know, and then ascending little by little as by steps, up to understanding of the most complex; and indeed designating an order among those which do not naturally go in order with respect to one another"].[2]

As analysis of these two texts suggests, in L'Astrée as a whole there is not only difference and alternation between two modes of thought but also a certain measure of exchange between them. In this way, for example, Hylas's and Tyrcis's analogical debate contains one reference to the "régles de l'art," which might permit the participants to overcome the limitations of purely analogically based thinking. Tyrcis acknowledges an epistemological gap between word and thing, between thought and expression, suggesting that the tongue (or, indeed, language) cannot "bien exprimer ce que le coeur ne peut entierement gouster." Similarly, one of Léonide's general principles favors nature over art, suggesting that "les choses que nature produict, sont toujours plus parfaictes que celles qui procedent de l'art, de mesme l'amour qui vient par inclination est plus grande et plus estimable que celle qui procede du dessein ou de l'obligation." This is itself an otherwise unsupported analogical view, but one which expresses a backward-looking, pre-Cartesian principle.

As might be expected, such issues are debated elsewhere in the five long volumes of *L'Astrée* also. Some references to the paradigm of sympathies and antipathies have already been quoted. In yet other passages the same Hylas shows a rudimentary understanding of the principle of constant variation when he declares that "Si aymer le contraire de ce que l'on a aymé est inconstance, et si la laideur est le contraire de la beauté, il n'y a point de doute que celuy conclut fort bien, qui soustient celuy estre inconstant, qui ayant aymé un beau visage, continue de l'aymer quand il est laid. Ceste consideration m'a fait croire, que pour n'estre inconstant, il faut aymer, tousjours et en tous lieux la beauté, et que lors qu'elle se separe de quelque subjet, on s'en doit de mesme separer d'amitié . . . " ["If it is inconstancy to love the opposite of what one has loved, and if ugliness is the opposite of beauty, there can be no doubt that one concludes very well in arguing that someone is inconstant if he has loved a beautiful face and continues to love it if it becomes ugly. This consideration has led me to believe that, in order not to be inconstant, one must love always and everywhere beauty, and if it separates itself from some subject, then one must similarly break off one's friendship . . . "].

Elsewhere, Ligdamon explains, in a manner suggestive of Léonide's—or Descartes's—system of classification, that "les extremes desirs ne sont point contre la raison: car n'est-il pas raisonnable de desirer toutes choses bonnes, selon le degré de leur bonté? Et par ainsi une extreme beauté sera raisonnablement aimée en extremité . . . " ["extreme desires are not contrary to reason; for is it not reasonable to desire all good things according to the degree of their goodness? And thus an extreme beauty will reasonably be loved extremely . . . "]. In a passage reminiscent of Charron and suggestive of La Rochefoucauld, Silvandre explains that "le prix, belle nymphe, qui est en toutes les choses de l'univers, ne se doit pas prendre pour ce que nous en voyons, mais pour ce à quoy elles sont propres. . . . Et par ceste raison, je veux dire, que pour cognoistre le prix de chacun, il faut regarder à quoy les dieux s'en servent, car il n'y a pas d'apparence, qu'ils ne sçachent bien la valeur de chaque chose" ["the price, beautiful nymph, which is in all the things of the universe, should not be taken to be what we see of it, but as that for which they are destined. . . . And for this reason I mean that to know the price of things, one must look at what the gods use them for, for it is not likely that they do not know very well the value of each thing"].[3]

Moreover, *L'Astrée* is well supplied with comments on the interaction of resemblance and reason. Thus the shepherdess Diane explains that it is not reasonable that "jamais la raison ne contrarie au devoir" ["reason never contradicts duty"] (1: 244). The sage Druid Adamas explains in some detail that it is God's will not only that "les choses insensibles, encores que contraires, soient unies et entretenues ensemble par liens d'amour, mais les sensibles et raisonnables aussi" ["inanimate things, even though contrary, be united and held together by bonds of love, but the perceptible and reasonable ones also"] (3: 217). This is why, explains Adamas, "aux elemens insensibles, il a donné des qualités qui les lient ensemble par sympathie; aux animaux, l'amour et le desir de perpetuer leur espece; aux hommes, la raison qui leur apprend à aimer Dieu en ses creatures, et les creatures en Dieu. Or, cette raison nous enseigne que tout ce qui est aimable se doit aimer selon les degrez de sa bonté, et, par ainsi, ce qui en aura plus, devra aussi estre plus aimé" ["to the inanimate things, he has given qualities which link them together by sympathy; to the animate, love and the desire to perpetuate their species; to men, reason which teaches them to love God in His creatures, and the creatures in God. Now, reason teaches that everything lovable should be loved according to the degree of its goodness, and thus, that which has more should also be more loved"] (3: 217–18). And Célidée asserts, perhaps more confidently than Montaigne or Charron would have, that she can never belong to Calidon, since "la nature me le deffend, et la raison aussi, qui n'est jamais contraire à la nature" ["nature forbids me to do it, and reason also, which is never contrary to nature"] (2: 63).

THE WEALTH of discussion of sensory impressions, sympathies, laws, judgment, reason, and epistemological issues in *L'Astrée* may well be taken as further evidence of some kind of Kuhnian epistemological crisis in the last decades of the sixteenth century and the first decades of the seventeenth. At the same time, however, *L'Astrée*'s second epistemological mode, as exemplified by the judgment of Léonide, may well represent something like a Kuhnian "new paradigm" and its influence on what he calls the "structure of scientific revolutions." For just as any

Malherbian poetic reform may appear to the historian to predate and develop in some measure independently of Malherbe, so any Cartesian revolution here appears to develop before and thus independently of Descartes. Indeed, in the pages of *L'Astrée,* the "Cornelian conflict" and "Cornelian love" celebrated in the theater of the *Grand Siècle* already appear, notably in the *ordonnances* of Léonide.

Any movement from the epistemology of Hylas and Tyrcis to that of Léonide may correspond, morever, to one of the psychological transformations described by Jean Piaget as that from a relatively childlike "réalisme substantiviste" to "l'explication par les relations géométriques et cinématiques," that is, by the selection of salient (geometric or kinetic) factors and evaluation of events according to their place on a value scale. Love, so often mystical or poetic in *L'Astrée,* may thus also become an object of physiological investigation—as, for example, when a healer who wishes to know who Calidon loves arranges that "toutes les jeunes bergeres . . . le vinssent visiter separement. . . . Et quant à luy, il luy tenoit tousjours le bras, et sans faire semblant de rien luy touchoit le pouls, pour cognoistre quand il prendroit quelque émotion" ["all the young shepherdesses . . . came to visit him separately. . . . And as for him (the healer), he held his arm the whole time, and without letting on took his pulse to find out when he might feel some strong emotion"].[4]

For similar reasons, the novel's two epistemological modes clearly lend confirmation to the theories of Michel Foucault. For like the almost exactly contemporary *Don Quixote* as analyzed in *Les Mots et les choses, L'Astrée*'s heterogeneous epistemological assumptions might well be interpreted as a moment of transition between two *épistémès*—or, more simply, between two sets of epistemological assumptions. However, if *L'Astrée* may confirm some epistemological coexistence or transition, it certainly does not confirm any sudden, overwhelming, quasi-structuralist transition. The later volumes of *L'Astrée,* appearing nearly twenty years after the first, are not fundamentally different in this respect from their predecessors. *L'Astrée* is, moreover, a very influential work. Read avidly across the whole seventeenth century, *L'Astrée*'s epistemological issues are echoed, reprised, expressed, and worked out in a very large number of works published during the following decades. The evolution of French poetry during this period might be adduced, among many other examples.[5] And most of the works studied in the following chapters deal, in one way or another, with similar epistemological issues.[6]

NOTES

1. Honoré d'Urfé, *L'Astrée,* ed. H. Vaganay, 5 vols. (Lyon: Masson, 1925), 1: 12, 22; 3: 229; citations are henceforth given in the text.

2. In Descartes, *Oeuvres et lettres,* pp. 137–38, 169.

3. D'Urfé, *L'Astrée,* 1: 96, 240–41; 2: 127. See Chapter 3 herein.

4. Piaget, *La Causalité physique chez l'enfant,* p. 284; d'Urfé, *L'Astrée,* 2: 35.

5. An earlier version of the present work included a rigorously chronological study of such words as "reason," "law," and the like in Malherbe and Saint-Amant. However different these two poets may appear in other respects, they show similar evolution with respect to these words, as do Mathurin Régnier and their contemporaries generally. To whatever extent the principles presented in the present study may have general application, an indefinite number of additional examples might be offered. In particular, some additional chapter—among all those which might be presented—might choose to study differences between Saint-Amant's early *Solitude,* which includes a description of Renaissance or baroque poetic furor, and Saint-Amant's slightly later *Le Contemplateur,* which expresses a strikingly more intellectualized conception of poetry and pays hommage to the new science as well. *La Solitude* contains one variant involving the word "law," moreover. In an early published version of the poem, Saint-Amant evokes the horrifying, no doubt baroque skeleton of a suicidal lover and writes:

> Aussi le ciel juge équitable
> Pour punir ceste cruauté
> Prononça contre sa beauté
> Une sentence épouvantable.

This relatively personalized image of equitable justice is modified significantly in the later published edition of *La Solitude,* however. In the second version, the same stanza reads:

> Aussi le ciel juge équitable
> Qui maintient les loix en vigueur
> Prononça contre sa rigueur
> Une sentence épouvantable.

See J. Lagny, *Le Poète Saint-Amant* (Paris: Nizet, 1964), pp. 52–65, and J. Bailbé and J. Lagny, eds., *Oeuvres,* 1 (Paris: Didier, 1971), p. 40.

6. One other striking novelistic example is the conclusion of another long seventeenth-century novel, one of the many versions of Gomberville's *Polexandre,* whose last volume was published in 1645. Gomberville writes that he is not displeased with his work's length and meandering course because—in terms reminiscent of the debates between Hylas, Tyrcis, and Léonide and her shepherdesses:

Un grand dessein ne me desplait pas, pource qu'il est bien tost imaginé: mais l'execution m'en est insupportable, pource qu'il y faut beaucoup de temps, beaucoup d'attention, beaucoup de servitude, et beaucoup d'ordre. Je n'ay jamais eu d'aversion pour les belles femmes. Cependant j'aime si fort la negligence et l'inegalité, que je trouve à redire en toutes celles qui sont tousjours si concertées, si regulieres, et si exactes en leurs ajustemens, qu'on les prend pour des peintures du pont Nostre Dame, plutost que pour des beautez vivantes. Leurs yeux, leurs pas, leurs ris, leurs discours, sont composez avec une rigoureuse symétrie. Leur gorge est ouverte avec plus d'art et de mesure, que celle d'un Bastion. Autant de fois qu'elles s'habillent, elles ont besoin de tous les instrumens d'un Mathematicien pour trouver les longitudes et les latitudes de leurs garcettes, et de leurs mouches: et il n'est si subtil Geometre, qui pût rencontrer en toutes les boucles de leurs cheveux, le moindre deffaut contre la definition du cercle. L'irregularité de mon esprit ne peut souffrir ces importunes et perpetuelles justesses.

[A great project does not displease me, since it can be imagined quickly. But the execution is unbearable for me, because it takes a lot of time, a lot of concentration, a lot of work, and a great deal of order. I have never been adverse to beautiful women. However, I am so fond of negligence and inequality that I find something to criticize in all those who are always so done up, so regular, and so exact in their outfits that one might take them for paintings of the Notre Dame bridge, rather than for living beauties. Their eyes, their step, their laughter, their conversation, are composed with a rigorous symmetry. Their bosom is opened with more art and measure than the opening of a bastion. Each time they dress, they need all the instruments of a mathematician to find the longitudes and latitudes of their pins and their mouches. And there is no geometer so subtle, that he can find in any of the curls of their hair the least fault against the definition of the circle. The irregularity of my mind cannot stand these perpetual and importunate exactnesses.] (Paris, 1645; 5: 611–14).

CHAPTER 5

Two Practical Manuals of a Noble Art: Henri de Saint-Didier and Girard Thibault

ANY TRANSFORMATION as general as that posited by Michel Foucault could be expected to have effects in a wide variety of—if indeed not all —intellectual domains. Foucault himself suggests, of course, that the new *épistémè* of 1605 revolutionized life sciences, linguistic science, economics, and literature; other works by the same author suggest that the same transformation may have altered conceptions of penology, cliniology, human folly, and human sexuality as well. Such a hypothesis finds both apparent contradiction and apparent confirmation, curiously, in a domain presumably far removed from the mainstream of intellectual preoccupation, namely the similarly inspired and yet very different works of Henri de Saint-Didier and Girard Thibault. The former is the author of a *Traicté contenant les secrets du premier livre sur l'espée seule, mere de toutes armes,* first published in 1573. The latter, apparently a fencing master to René Descartes among others, is the author of an *Académie de l'espée,* published with magnificent, engraved illustrations in 1628.

In Saint-Didier's time as in our own, one might reasonably entertain doubts about the feasibility of learning fencing from a book. Yet, as Henri-Jean Martin points out in his extensive study of early French publishing, the period was characterized by social conflict, social movement, and the appearance of newly armed or newly landed families who were apparently enthusiastic readers and customers for self-help manuals on a variety of practical subjects. Saint-Didier appears tacitly to acknowledge the difficulties of verbal description of sword-play when he begins his treatise with a eulogy of "l'experience des choses" ["the experience of things"] and judgment, which operates "tant par raison que par effait" ["as much by reason as by result"]. In addition to these commonplaces of any age, however, a part of the knowledge Saint-Didier seeks to present is of a kind that a modern fencing coach might see as eminently impractical—that is, knowledge of an analogical or a metaphorical type. Thus Saint-Didier explains his preference for the low or hanging guard in fencing with the possibly uncombat-oriented reasoning that, "attendu que toutes choses se commencent aux fondements: comme pour exemple ... les maçons quand ils viennent à commencer à bastir les maisons, ne commencent pas à la tuille ... " ["since everything begins at the foundations: as for example ... masons, when they come to begin to build houses, do not begin with the roof-tiles ... "]. In the same way Saint-Didier's treatise ends with a detailed and essentially metaphorical comparison of fencing with tennis. According to the author, his analogy is not meant for experts, only for beginners. In the beginner's context, he states, the attacks of fencing and tennis are similar, except for the *estoc,* or thrust, since the tennis racquet has no point. Otherwise, a good racquet is to tennis what a good sword is to fencing, both activities involve give and take, and so on, so that "la paulme et lesdites armes, comme dit est, ont une grande affinité" ["tennis and said arms, as has been said, have a great affinity"].[1]

At the same time, however, Saint-Didier's account is not composed exclusively of metaphorical observations. Quite clearly, even if one were to accept the idea that Foucaldian *mathesis* and classification or Cartesian analytic geometry are characteristic of a later age, it cannot be shown that all of mathematics, or all classification, or every application of *mathesis* to practical matters began abruptly in the time of Malherbe or Descartes. In the time of Saint-Didier, even the most mystical or poetic of fencers was aware that certain distinguishing principles were of fundamental importance in the noble art of fencing, that a certain repertoire of attacks and defenses had its role to play. Indeed, a good many passages of Saint-Didier's *Traicté* might appear to go somewhat further than the minimum in classifying and hierarchizing the elements of his subject—conceivably making Saint-Didier something like a classicist theoretician of fencing, some fifty years ahead of his time.

Thus he writes that his treatise is an instrument of order against disorder. He allies himself in his dedicatory epistle with "ceux qui taschans (comme l'on dit) ayder voire parfaire la nature, on reduist les choses confuses en ordres, et de telle sorte que ce que de prime-face sembloit rude, malaisé, et inaccessible, a esté par eux rendu aisé, traictable, et facile à aborder: veu mesmement que le seul mal ... provient de la confusion et desordre des choses ... " ["those who, trying (as they say) to aid or indeed perfect nature, have reduced confused things to order, and in such a way that what at first seemed rude, difficult, and inaccessible, has been rendered by them easy, understandable, and easy to undertake: given in the same way that only evil . . . comes from confusion and disorder of things . . . "].[2]

Elsewhere, as the author explains various aspects of fencing, including the *coup d'essai,* strategies for disarming an adversary, and the dancelike footwork accompanying each stroke, he observes that the repertoire of attacks in fencing is limited. "Quant au premier poinct," he writes, "c'est à sçavoir combien il y a de desmarches: Je respond qu'il n'y en a que deux, par ce que nous n'avons que deux pieds" ["As for the first point, namely how many movements there are: I answer that there are only two, because we have only two feet"]. Saint-Didier tells how, arguing with a group of foreigners, he asked them how many blows there were. They answered, "plusieurs" ["several"]. The purist or classicist Saint-Didier responded disdainfully that "toute response infinie n'a point de certitude" ["no infinite response can be certain"]. One of the foreigners reflects further and decides there are five attacks, but this is still too many for Saint-Didier, who concludes the conversation: "Quant à moy, je dis avec les doctes, que ce qui ce [*sic*] peut faire avec peu, est meilleur que ce qui ce [*sic*] fait avec beaucoup" ["As for me, I say with the wise, that what can be done with little is better than what is done with much"].[3]

If Henri de Saint-Didier is a proponent of limited repertoires and classical economy, his successor Girard Thibault might appear to many as a relatively more baroque author. Dedicating his book to the "tresaugustes, treshaults, trespuissants, tresillustres, haults, magnifiques, Empereur, Roys, Princes, Ducs, Comtes et touts autres seigneurs et nobles fauteurs et amateurs de la tresnoble science de manier les armes" ["very august, very high, very powerful, very illustrious, high, magnificent Emperor, Kings, Princes, Dukes, Counts, and all other lords and noble practicers and students of the very noble science of wielding arms"], Thibault retains the Renaissance notion that the human body "contient un abbregé, non seulement de tout ce qu'on voit icy bas en terre, mais encores de ce qui est au ciel mesme; representant le tout avec une harmonie, si douce, belle, et entiere, et avec une si juste convenance de Nombres, Mesures, et Poids, qui se rapportent si merveilleusement aux vertus des Quatre Elements, et aux influences des Planetes, qu'il ne s'en trouve nulle autre semblable" ["contains a summary, not only of everything to be seen here below on earth, but also of what is in the sky itself; representing the whole with so sweet, beautiful, and complete a harmony, and with so exact an accord of Numbers, Measures, and Weights, which are so marvelously related to the virtues of the Four Elements and to the influences of the Planets, that there is no other like it"]. Elsewhere he speaks explicitly of "ce Microcosme du corps humain" ["this Microcosm of the human body"].[4]

The basis of Thibault's system is the quasi-mystical, quasi-analogical, but also, presumably, geometrical figure of the circle. At the end of a long development on the subject, Thibault writes that "Pour conclusion, le Cercle c'est le fondement de la Science des Armes; c'est celuy qui nous descouvre touts les dangers, qui se peuvent presenter par tout le discours [sic] d'une bataille; guide de nos mouvements, adresse des intentions, asseurance des pas . . . duquel on se servira parmy les perilleuses vagues de cest Exercice, comme les Matelots de la bussole, et d'une bonne carte Marine . . ." ["In conclusion, the Circle is the foundation of the Science of Arms; it is that which uncovers all dangers for us, among those which appear in the course of a battle; guides our movements, intelligence of intentions, assurance of step . . . which we shall use among the perilous waves of this Exercise as the Sailor the compass, or a good Marine map . . ."]. A series of other metaphors follows. Elsewhere, Thibault explains that his view of the circle and the proportions of the human body are comparable to those of Albrecht Dürer's second book of proportions, folio sixty-one of the well-known Renaissance portrayals of the human body inscribed in a circle, and an image that might appear slightly out of date in the France of Louis XIII, Descartes, and the three musketeers.[5]

Thibault is not unaware, moreover, of the virtues of the bizarre and surprising. He counsels studying and using unlikely tactics in fencing, asking rhetorically: "Mais quoy donc? Direz vous, ce sont des occasions inutiles, pour ce qu'elles sont rares? Au contraire, le [sic] plus estranges se sont les plus necessaires. Car l'Ennemy ne manquera pas à faire une action estrange, s'il pense qu'il vous en mettra en desordre . . . " ["But what do you mean, will you say that these are useless opportunities because they are rare? On the contrary, the strangest ones are the most necessary. For the Enemy will not fail to use a strange action, if he thinks it will put you in disarray . . . "]. At the same time, however, Thibault is aware of the limitations of certain aspects of the Renaissance, or, possibly, baroque worldview—at least as it may apply to fencing.

Thus he discusses the weaknesses of a world of resemblance, writing that "Quand les Medecins font leurs visites, pour asseoir un bon jugement, il n'y a chose au Monde qui les trouble d'avantage, que la similitude d'une maladie à l'autre . . . " ["When doctors make their examinations, in order to arrive at a correct judgment, there is nothing in the world which causes more trouble than the resemblance of one malady to another . . . "]. Where Saint-Didier compared fencing to tennis, Thibault compares his subject, in a passage which may recall the critiques of all thought by Montaigne or Charron, to rhetoric or jurisprudence:

> . . . comme les accusations sont sujettes aux exceptions, les exceptions aux repliques, les repliques aux duplications, triplications, et finalement à toutes les Instances que la partie adverse voudra faire; ainsi au fait des armes il n'y a aucun trait tant ordinaire, tant bien examiné, tant prisé, tant secret, ne tant admirable, qui n'ait son contraire; de sorte qu'il ne se faut jamais fier en aucun trait particulier . . .
>
> [. . . just as the accusations are subject to exceptions, the exceptions to replies, the replies to duplications, triplications, and finally to all the stipulations the adverse party may wish to make, so in the world of combat there is no trick, whether ordinary, whether carefully studied, whether highly valued, or secret, or admirable, that does not have its opposite, so that one must never rely on any single special trick . . .].[6]

Like his predecessor, Thibault is aware of some of the anomalies involved in trying to teach fencing through a book, even a beautifully illustrated one. Thus he warns his reader at one point that theory and practice are very different. He explains his preference for the straight guard as "la plus noble, et la plus parfaite, de toutes" ["the noblest and most perfect of all"] but adds:

> s'il est question de tirer les armes par courtoisie, celuy qui sçaura bien presenter la droite ligne, n'[aura] besoin de nulle autre pour sa defense. . . . Mais quand il seroit question de tirer à bon, et sur tout quand il y iroit de la vie, il n'y a nulle garde, haute ne basse, longue ne courte, nulle posture de corps, nulle tenue d'espee, et fust elle qualifiée de touts les avantages possibles en laquelle on se doive arrester pour attendre. Il est vray, que ce livre est grandement rempli des postures de la droite ligne; mais ce n'est que pour donner instruction. Quand ce viendra à l'a [sic] Pratique, je veux que nostre Escholier abandonne tout cela . . .

[if it is a matter of drawing weapons chivalrously, he who knows how to present the straight line will need nothing further for his defense. . . . But if it is a question of drawing in real combat, and especially in a matter of life and death, there is no guard, high or low, long or short, no posture of the body, no sword grip, not even if it had every possible advantage, in which one should stop and wait. It is true that this book is full of straight-line postures; but this is only to give instruction. When it comes to practical situations, I want our pupil to forget all that . . .].

In order to win in fencing, Thibault explains, one must gain an advantage. And one cannot gain an advantage if one rests in an attitude of beautiful symmetry: "Il le faut aborder plus pres," he writes, "pour le mettre en danger; mais avec asseurance, Bon pied, bon oeil" ["you have to move in close to put him in danger; but with assurance, with solid footwork and a good eye"].[7]

At the same time, however, any analogical or numerological or possibly baroque aspects of the Thibault school of fencing are only a part of the exposition. The long title of Thibault's work is *Académie de l'espée . . . ou se demonstrent par reigles mathematiques sur le fondement d'un cercle mysterieux la theorie et pratique des vrais et jusqu'a present incognus secrets du maniement des armes a pied et a cheval.* And whereas Saint-Didier's text and diagrams were perhaps most suggestive of instruction in the dance, Thibault's text and diagrams clearly suggest a mathematical analysis, a geometry of fencing. Thibault's circle is described as "mysterieux" in his title and compared to Dürer's man inscribed in a circle in the text; however, Thibault's circle is also a practical figure, which he encourages his reader to inscribe on the floor and walk about in:

Ceux qui seront curieux d'examiner ces calculations de plus pres, les trouveront assez accordantes aux regles de la Mathematique; et pour ceux qui n'en quierent que la simple Pratique, ils en pourront prendre la mesure sur le terroir avec un baston de la longeur du Diametre parti en 24. Nombres, et chascun d'iceux nombres en 10. parties, et les parties en 10. minutes.

[Those who may wish to examine these calculations more closely will find them more or less in agreement with the rules of mathematics; and for those who seek only practical knowledge, they can measure this out on the ground with a stick of the length of the diameter divided into twenty-four numbers, and each one of these numbers into ten parts, and the parts into ten minutes].[8]

Thibault believes that the correct sword length is the distance from the swordsman's feet to his navel, apparently somewhat short by seventeenth-century as well as by modern standards. Thibault gives a list of reasons why the shorter sword is preferable, however. Not only is it easier to carry and faster to draw, but it also is easier and faster to use at close quarters—which, for Thibault, constitutes the essence of fencing. His diagram divides the sword blade into twelve parts—Thibault's way of expressing as a graduated scale the classic fencing notion of "strong" and "weak" parts of the blade. He explains that differences in the height of the swordsmen may modify somewhat the dimensions of his circle, but explains that henceforth the circle of an average person will be shown in the diagrams.

If an average person is to be the model for the fencer's circle, Thibault further suggests that a mathematically based model is inherently desirable:

> Toutes personnes de jugement confessent, qu'il seroit fort à desiderer pour l'adresse de l'Exercice des Armes, qu'il y eust une certaine et inviolable Mesure, selon laquelle on peust regler exactement toutes les Distances, et à l'advenant aussi touts les mouvements, grands et petits, tardifs et vistes.

> [All men of judgment agree that it would be most desirable for dexterity in the exercise of arms, that there be a precise and inviolable measure, according to which all distances, and indeed all movements, small and large, late and rapid, may be regulated].[9]

When it comes to describing specific attacks and parries, Thibault's style is strikingly different from his predecessor's. Thus Saint-Didier, not totally a stranger to geometry himself, nevertheless describes an essentially nongeometrical situation: "Icy est monstré la garde et tenue pour faire deux bons et subtils coups, en la mainiere de triangle, et quadriangle, pour le Lieutenant assaillant, contre le Prevost deffendant ... dont ont tous deux soubs leurs pieds le portrait et figure d'iceluy pour le bien faire" ["Here is shown the guard and posture to make two good and subtle attacks, in the manner of the triangle and quadrangle, for the Lieutenant attacking against the Prevost defending ... of whom both have under their feet the portrait and figure of (their footwork) in order to execute it properly"]. Thibault, in a similar description, adopts a very different descriptive system:

Premiere operation. Alexandre s'estant preallablement avancé deux ou trois pas devers le Cerele [*sic:* circle?] N. 1 en plantant le pied gauche en terre, il a mis l'espee en angle aigu à son costé droit, ce qu'estant fait, il hausse le pied droit en dehors, comme aussi le bras avec l'espee, les mettant en angle obtus. . . .

[First operation. Alexandre, having first advanced two or three steps across the circle, has placed the sword at an acute angle to his right side, which having done, he raises the right foot outside, and at the same time the arm with the sword, placing them in an obtuse angle . . .].[10]

In general, Thibault's fencing system and description system are based almost entirely on the notion that certain mathematically determined points within the circle are the correct or "strong" ones from which to make certain movements and that certain sword angles are the correct ones to gain an advantage in certain situations—most often by moving inside the opponent's guard. The result is a description, not of two facing dancers, but of two opposing geometries.

Thibault views his fencing treatise, containing two books of thirty-three and thirteen engravings each, in most cases with six or a dozen situations depicted per engraving, as nevertheless a reductive one. Space has permitted him to present only the principal precepts of his art:

Si on me dit, qu'il y a bien encores des autres occasions, dont les particularitez n'ont pas esté representées, Je respons, qu'il n'est ny besoin, ny possible de ce faire, non plus que de comter les sablons de la mer, car les changements sont infinis: la teste, le bras, l'espee, le pied, un peu plus avancé, ou retiré, plus haut, ou plus bas, ou à costé, ce sont tousjours des changements, mais non pas tousjours d'importance en sorte qu'il faille estrendre [*sic*] les preceptes si avant.

[If someone says that there are a great many other situations, whose details have not been presented, I answer that it is not necessary, nor possible to do so, no more than to count the grains of sand of the sea, for the modifications are infinite: the head, the arm, the sword, the foot, a little farther forward, or back, higher, or lower, or to the side, all these are changes, but not always important ones such that one must go further into the matter.]

If the possible positions in fencing are infinite, Thibault is content, nevertheless, with reduction to a manageable number. Toward the end of his first book, he returns to the reductive nature of its presentation. He writes, in a very different spirit than, for example, Montaigne:

> ... comme un legislateur se contente de donner quelques loix, afin que selon icelles, non seulement les differents à l'occasion desquels elles sont fondées puissent estre decidez, mais aussi ceux qui ne different que de circonstances, et qui ne changent point l'essence du subject: aussi, nous pour terminer un nombre infini d'operations ...

> [... just as a legislator is pleased to make a few laws, so that in the light of these not only the cases which gave rise to them can be decided, but also those which are only different in circumstances, and which do not change the essence of the subject (can be decided as well): in the same way, we ourselves, in order to treat an infinite number of operations ...].

Thibault thus chooses to apply a reductive principle. And in this light, Thibault's *Académie de l'espée* is not only a mathematization of its subject but also a classicization as well, containing both analogical and "logical" elements presented in a kind of synthesis attained through the creation of rules and reduction to average or exemplary situations.[11]

Henri-Jean Martin documents in his *Livres, pouvoirs et société à Paris au XVIIᵉ siècle* how the period saw tremendous expansion in the publication of practical manuals of all kinds. The evidence suggests, moreover, that the kind of analysis presented here might also be applied to pairs of practical manuals in a wide variety of domains. One thinks of Abraham Bosse's treatise of 1667, significantly entitled the *Peintre converty aux règles de son art*, Charles Estienne's *Maison rustique* of 1564, and Vinet and Mizaud's *Maison champestre* of 1607.[12]

Another striking example might be drawn from the world of gamesmanship. The anonymous *Mort aux pipeurs* of 1608, "*Où sont contenuës toutes les tromperies et piperies du jeu, et le moyen de les eviter*" [in which are contained all the tricks and snares of gaming, and the ways to avoid them] appears innocent of Cartesian intent. Its unknown author embraces the baroque image of the thinking—and writing—process when he warns against trying to write on very general subjects. He explains that "l'esprit humain[,] pour quelque force qu'il ayt, [est] impuissant pour ce porter à desbroüiller un tel cahos [*sic*] et confusion de choses diverses et infinies." In partial contrast Charles Sorel's *Maison des jeux* of 1642 mixes fictional narrative and dialogue with systematic presentation of a large number of existing games—those inventions of wit and conversation that seem to have been an essential facet of seventeenth-century salon life. Sorel describes games of analogy, like rebuses, or the "Jeu des Signes," or the "Jeu des choses qui conviennent ensemble," or the "Jeu de la Similitude." He also describes, however, games of a more scientific or "repertoirizing" bent, like the "Jeu des Mathematiques," or the "Jeu du Bastiment et du Jardinage," or the "Jeu de la Beauté ou de la Laideur," or the "Jeu des Sciences et des Arts." Sorel's very remarkable treatise precedes by twelve years the first edition of La Marinière's *La Maison académique*, celebrated in the history of gamesmanship as the first modern codification of the rules of games—that is, the classification, the normatization, and the mathematization of such games as checkers, chess, backgammon, and card games.[13]

One other striking example is the field of manuals of sexual activity. While modern histories of the "marriage manual" customarily point to such ancient authors as Ovid or Aretino, no systematic manual of sexual practice appears in the Occident until the seventeenth century. Sorel's Romanesque hero Francion calls for a manual describing the "plus mignards jeux de l'amour" in 1623, although neither Francion nor Sorel apparently actually wrote one. The following decades, however, saw at least two such manuals—Nicolas Chorier's celebrated *Dialogues* or *Académie des dames* of 1659 and Michel Millot's (or Mililot's) *Escole des filles* of 1655.[14]

Millot announces in a prefatory epistle that his book is essentially a regularization, that is, a kind of mathematization of its subject. The *Escole des filles* is simply "le recueil des principales choses que vous devez sçavoir pour contenter vos maris quand vous en aurez; c'est le secret infaillible pour vous faire aimer des hommes quand vous ne series pas belles, et le moyen aysé de couler en douceur et en plaisirs tout le temps de vostre jeunesse" ["a compendium of the principal things you should know to satisfy your husbands when you have them; it is the infallible secret to make yourself loved by men even if you are not beautiful, and a way of spending sweetly and pleasurably all the time of your youth"]. In such a book sexuality becomes an object of classification, a means of specifically progressive and, to stretch a term, Cartesian arousal. Seeing love in terms of a repertoire of sexual possibilities— perfumes, objects, dialogue, positions, and movements—it prefigures such determined and, perhaps, maniacally extensive classifications as the *120 Jours de Sodome* or indeed the *Psychopathia sexualis*. Millot emphasizes the importance of learning "la theorie avant la pratique" ["theory before practice"] in sex—where, he states, "il faut que tout se fasse dans les reigles du plaisir" ["everything must be done according to the rules of pleasure"].[15]

Certainly most far-reaching in their implications, however, are those seventeenth-century practical manuals that sought to give instruction in the manipulation of language and thought itself. One might wish to compare, say the 1572 *Grammaire* of Ramus with the well-known, trail-blazing gammar of Vaugelas. Or one might wish to compare Ramus's *Dialectique* of 1555 with Arnauld and Nicole's pivotal *Logique,* the so-called *Logique de Port-Royal* of 1662.[16]

Treating a subject whose essential principles were laid out long before by Aristotle, Ramus is perhaps most notable in the history of logic for the attention he pays to "extralogical" values, remarking finally that "pour avoir le vray loz de logique, n'est pas asses de sçavoir caqueter en l'eschole des reigles d'icelle, mais il les fault exercer et pratiquer es poëtes, orateurs, philosophes, c'est à dire en toute espece d'esprit: en considerant et examinant leurs vertus et vices, en imitant premierement par escripture et par voix leur bonne invention et disposi- tion . . . " ["to have true knowledge of logic, it is not enough to know how to cackle in school about the rules of it; instead one must practice and frequent the poets, orators, and philosophers, that is, every sort of mind. One must consider and examine their virtues and vices, imitating in writing and speaking their good invention and disposition . . . "]—the last two being rhetorical rather than logical terms. Ramus deliberately chooses his examples of different types of syllogisms among the poets of his day—Ronsard, Marot, Pasquier, Du Bellay, and the like—even though, as he remarks, poets are wont to present their syllogisms in the wrong order, or to skip steps in their argument, "suyvantz l'usage naturel, encore quilz traictent questions syllogistiques . . . " ["following natural usage, even though they treat syllogistic questions . . . "].[17]

Arnauld and Nicole, in contrast, see their subject as a function of classification. As the *Logique* states in its introductory discourse, "La vraie raison place toutes choses dans le rang qui leur convient" ["True reason places each thing in the rank which is appropriate to it"]. The best way to avoid error, the *Logique* suggests, is to have "des regles pour s'y conduire de telle sorte, que la recherche de la verité en fût et plus facile et plus sûre; et ces regles sans doute ne sont pas impossibles" ["rules so as to proceed in such a way that seeking truth would be both easier and surer; and such rules are no doubt not impossible"]. Owing a considerable and obvious debt to Descartes as well as to Pascal, the *Logique de Port Royal* deliberately chooses its examples of various syllogisms among the sciences of rhetoric, moral philosophy, physics, metaphysics, and geometry, a choice with implications for the hierarchy of different branches of knowledge in the following decades, as subsequent chapters suggest.[18]

NOTES

1. Saint-Didier, *Traicté...* (Paris: J. Mettayer, 1573; rpt. ed. Soc. du livre d'Art Ancien et Moderne, 1907), fols. 2 r°, 3 r°, 4 v°, 89 v°.

2. Ibid., fol. 2 r°.

3. Ibid., fols. 3 v°, 6 v°–7 r°.

4. Thibault, *Académie de l'espée* (Brussels, 1628), dedication, Livre Iᵉʳ, Tableau I, pp. 1, 4.

5. Ibid., Liv. Iᵉʳ, Tab. I, pp. 13–14.

6. Ibid., Liv. Iᵉʳ, Tab. XI, p. 1; XII, p. 1; XIII, p. 6.

7. Ibid., Liv. Iᵉʳ, Tab. IV, p. 4; VI, p. 6.

8. Ibid., Liv. Iᵉʳ, Tab. I, p. 12.

9. Ibid., Liv. Iᵉʳ, Tab. II, p. 1.

10. Saint-Didier, *Traicté,* fol. 52 v°–53 v°. Thibault, *Académie de l'espée,* Liv. Iᵉʳ, Tab. III, p. 5.

11. Thibault, *Académie de l'espée,* Liv. Iᵉʳ, Tab. XV, p. 1; XXXII, p. 6.

12. See Henri-Jean Martin, *Livre, pouvoirs et société à Paris au XVIIᶜ siècle* (Geneva: Droz, 1969), 1: 233–38, for example.

13. *Mort aux pipeurs* (Paris, 1608), Bibliothèque Nationale call number V47249—fol. 2 v°; Sorel, *La Maison des jeux* (Paris, 1642); La Marinière, *La Maison académique* (Paris, 1654).

14. Both in *Romanciers du XVIIᶜ siècle,* ed. A. Adam (Paris: Pléiade, 1958), pp. 321–22.

15. Mil[i]lot, *Ecole des filles* (Paris: Euredif, 1979), pp. 3, 49. In *La Volonté de savoir* (Paris: Gallimard, 1976), first volume of a projected *Histoire de la sexualité,* Michel Foucault treats intelligently but very incompletely the prodigious growth of discourse on sex in the later seventeenth century. Along with the first Western manuals of sexual practice, the same period also saw the origins of pornography as currently understood. A notable example from the abundant production of more or less badly written sexual adventures of the time is the anonymous *Adamite ou le jésuite insensible* of 1684. The *Adamite*'s only comic or

erotic interest depends squarely on the principles of classification, hierarchization, encoding, and *transcodage.* Seventeenth-century sex manuals and the *Adamite* are discussed more extensively in H. De Ley, " 'Dans les reigles du plaisir . . . ' Transformations of Sexual Knowledge in Seventeenth-Century France," in *Onze nouvelles études sur l'image de la femme,* ed. W. Leiner (Tubingen: G. Narr, 1984), pp. 25–32, reprinted in *French Literature Series* (Columbia: University of South Carolina Press, 1982). For other recent discussion, see Pierre Dormon, *Le Mythe de la procréation à l'âge baroque* (Paris: Pauvert, 1977), as well as a recent number of *Communications* devoted to *Sexualités occidentales* (35 [1982]).

16. Ramus's *Grammaire* and *Dialectique* have been reprinted as Pierre de la Ramée dit Ramus, *Gramere (1562). Grammaire (1572). Dialectique (1555)* (Geneva: Slatkine, 1972). The *Logique de Port-Royal,* which itself evolved through five states in fourteen editions between 1662 and 1685, has benefited from critical edition by Pierre Clair and François Girbal, *La Logique ou l'art de penser* (Paris: P.U.F., 1965). See also Gassendi, *Logicae,* and Louis Lesclache, *Philosophie* (1648), among others. For a general view see Robert Blanche, *La Logique et son histoire* (Paris: A. Colin, 1970). See Ong.

17. Ramus, *Dialectique,* pp. 114, 137–38; see pp. 61–65, 128–40. For Ramus's reputation as a poetic logician, see Blanche, *La Logique.* In some sense it may be that Ramus is the inventor of the method of the present study—Foucault and Kuhn notwithstanding et al.—that is, Ramus uses poetic examples to illustrate epistemological statements, thus inventing something like Greimas's "cognitive dimension" in literary studies as well.

18. Arnauld and Nicole, *Logique de Port-Royal,* pp. 18, 20. Whereas Ramus distinguishes between names that are and are not equivalent to the things designated (*Dialectique,* pp. 40–47, esp. pp. 46–47), Arnauld and Nicole dwell at some length on the arbitrary nature of language (pp. 41–43).

A very extensive treatment indeed would be required to do justice to the *Logique de Port-Royal*—or, likewise, certain other seventeenth-century practical or scientific treatises—in the context of the analysis presented in this chapter. A brilliant and elegant contribution to the subject is Louis Marin's *La Critique du discours* (Paris: Minuit, 1975), which takes as its point of departure the *Logique*'s famous distinction between definitions of names and definitions of things (*Logique,* p. 21, and Book 1, chs. 12, 13).

CHAPTER 6

Two Versions of a Tale of Two Cities: Schélandre's *Tyr et Sidon*

THE EPISTEMOLOGICAL ALTERNATIVES studied in the previous chapters are also reflected in the theater of the first decades of the seventeenth century. Histories of the period speak of a rapid rise in the importance of theatrical writing and production, accompanied moreover by intense theoretical controversy. Whether or not one might be tempted to attribute these rapid changes to some new *épistémè*, one of their results was frequent rewriting of already published works. Not only were certain traditional subjects reworked by new authors, but some dramatists modified their own works considerably, presumably to meet changes in taste. As is well known, Corneille extensively rewrote his plays of the 1620s and 1630s, sometimes explaining that when he began writing for the theater he didn't even know that rules existed. Montchrestien published three versions of his *Sophonisbe* in 1595, 1603, and 1604, explaining in another preface that he wanted to be like a painter who, "voulant tirer au vif la figure d'un prince, en ébauche grossièrement les premiers traits qui le font déjà reconnoître, mais après avoir ajouté les couleurs et conduit son ouvrage jusqu'à·perfection, ce semble être une autre chose, et néanmoins c'est la même chose" ["wanting to draw from life the face of a prince, sketches roughly the main lines which make him recognizable; but after he has added the colors and brought the work to perfection, it seems to be something else and nevertheless remains the same"]. And Jean de Schélandre published strikingly different—yet similar—versions of his *Tyr et Sidon* in 1608 and in 1628, twenty years later.[1]

Both texts tell approximately the same story. After long warfare between the two cities, a major battle has ended in a stalemate. In the course of battle, the Tyrian king's son Léonte and the Sidonian king's son Belcar have each been taken prisoner by the opposing sides. While the enlightened Sidonian king negotiates for peace with the bellicose Tyrian ruler, both sons are well treated in the opposing cities. Belcar recovers from his wounds and falls in love with the Tyrian princess, Méliane. Méliane is in love with Belcar, but so also is her older sister, Cassandre. Meanwhile, Léonte seduces the wife of a Sidonian citizen who, ignoring political implications, has Léonte murdered in the street by cutthroats. When the news of this unfortunate event reaches the Tyrian king, he vows vengeance on Belcar. However, Cassandre's nurse arranges an escape by sea. She leads Belcar to believe he is escaping with his beloved Méliane but substitutes Cassandre for Méliane in the departing ship.

The most obvious difference between the two plays is the ending of the intrigue described above. The 1608 version is a tragedy in the manner of such sixteenth-century writers as Garnier or Montchrestien. In keeping with the requirements of a tragic ending, Schélandre has Belcar jump overboard when he discovers he has escaped with Cassandre instead of Méliane. Cassandre stabs herself with Belcar's dagger. Her body floats to shore and Méliane finds it on the beach—just in time to be discovered with the body and with Belcar's dagger by the Tyrian king. Méliane is executed, and the Tyrian king, in his madness, stabs a courtier, who promptly kills him in return.

The 1628 version of *Tyr et Sidon* is a tragicomedy. As in the previous text, Cassandre kills herself, and Belcar and Méliane are arrested. However, witnesses arrive in time to recount the true course of events. Cassandre's nurse is punished, along with the Sidonian husband, thoughtfully delivered up by the Sidonian king. The Tyrian king is willing to listen to reason, and Méliane and Belcar's marriage consecrates lasting peace between the two cities, soon to be united under a single crown.

The second version moves decisively toward what T. J. Reiss has called the "dramatic illusion." The first text's chorus is eliminated in the later edition. And whereas the 1608 text groups its more than 3,000 alexandrines mostly into monologues, followed rather stiffly and mechanically by passages of stichomythia, the 1628 text alternates monologue and stichomythia with scenes of dramatic conflict and more naturally structured dialogue. Whereas the first approach links Schélandre to such authors as Garnier, Montchrestien, Chrétien des Croix, and Hardy, Schélandre's later technique is closer to Corneille and Corneille's principal rival in the third decade of the seventeenth century, Jean Mairet.[2]

Indeed, Schélandre adds something like Cornelian dramatic values to his second version—elements of psychological motivation and conflict of personal passion and the affairs of state. The difference is clearly visible even in the arguments of the two plays. In 1608, summarizing the action of the tragedy, Schélandre writes:

Tiribaze Roy de Tyr, et Aristarque Roy de Sidon, avoient une guerre continuelle ensemble, ou sur ces annees dernieres les Sidoniens avoient eu du pire. Advint qu'entre les deux terroirs ils donnerent une si furieuse bataille et tant opiniastrement disputee que la nuict venant les departit avec pareille perte de gens et égal advantage, de façon que les deux fils des Roys susdits qui conduisoient les armees (estants les peres des-ja vieux) furent faits prisonniers amenés à la Court de part et d'autre, et de là fut arrestée une tresve de six mois, durant laquelle se devoient traicter les conditions d'une ferme paix.

[Tiribaze, king of Tyr, and Aristarque, king of Sidon, were continually at war, and in recent years the Sidonians had had the worst of it. It happened that between their two territories they had so furiously and obstinately disputed a battle that when night came they separated with equal losses and equal advantage, in such a way that the two sons of the above-mentioned kings, which sons were leading the armies (since their fathers were already old), were made prisoners and taken to the opposing courts, and because of this a six-month truce was called to negotiate the conditions of a firm peace.]

Schélandre's 1628 argument describes the same situation in much more Cornelian terms:

Pharnabaze Roy de Tyr, et Abdolomin Roy de Sidon, apres s'estre faict la guerre l'un à l'autre par l'espace de dix ans avec des evenemens si variables qu'on ne pouvoit dire quel estoit le victorieux ou le vaincu, se resolurent d'en venir à un combat general, et de se choquer de toutes les forces de leurs Estats, pour voir enfin qui demeureroit le maistre. Les Tyriens donc sous la conduite de Leonte, et les Sidoniens sous celle de Belcar, fils des deux Roys, jeunes hommes pleins de courage, donnent bataille, où la fortune continuant à se joüer de ces peuples voulut que la perte fut esgalle, et que les deux chefs d'armée fussent pris en diverses rencontres et menez captifs par leurs ennemis, Belcar à Tyr, et Leonte à Sidon. Les deux peres touchez de mesme passion de joye et de tristesse, font tresve d'un commun consentement pour donner quelque ordre à leurs affaires, mais avec des intentions bien differentes: Car Pharnabaze, Prince encore vigoureux, en qui l'aage n'avoit pû esteindre ny amoindrir ceste ardeur guerriere et ceste haute ambition qui le possedoit dés sa jeunesse . . . mesprisoit son ennemy. . . .

Au contraire le bon Abdolomin s'essayoit par toutes voyes honnestes et legitimes de faire la paix . . .

[Pharnabaze, king of Tyr, and Abdolomin, king of Sidon, after having made war one against the other for the space of ten years with such mixed results that no one could say who was the victor or the vanquished, resolved to leave matters to a general combat, and to throw against each other all the forces of their States, to see who would remain the victor. The Tyrians therefore, under the leadership of Léonte, and the Sidonians under that of Belcar, sons of the two kings, young men full of courage, gave battle, wherein fortune, continuing to play with these two peoples, ordained that the losses would be equal and that the chiefs of the two armies would be taken in the various skirmishes and led off as captives, Belcar to Tyr and Léonte to Sidon. The two fathers, touched by the same passions of joy and sadness, made peace by common consent to get their affairs in order, but with very different intentions. For Pharnabaze, a still vigorous prince in whom age had not extinguished nor diminished the bellicose ardor and high ambition which had possessed him since his youth . . . scorned his enemy. . . . But on the contrary the good Abdolomin tried every honest and legitimate means of making peace . . .].[3]

Schélandre's 1628 argument thus adds that Léonte and Belcar are "jeunes hommes pleins de courage"; he adds that their two fathers were "touchez de mesme passion de joye et de tristesse"; and he adds further that the two kings consented to their truce with "des intentions bien differentes." Just as Schélandre adds psychological motivation and Cornelian conflict to his argument, moreover, he also adds some 1,700 lines to his second text, for a total of 4,818, presented in not one but two *journées*. The first play observes the three unities of time, place, and action as understood in the period with the exception of a single scene. Taking place in twenty-four hours, all the scenes but one are set in Tyre. Battles, negotiations, murders, escapes, and the rest are recited by a relatively small number of personages and messengers in a relatively small number of scenes. In the 1628 tragicomedy, however, battles and murders are presented onstage, with the consequent increase in the number of lines, decors, time lapses, and players. The first act moves freely and deliberately to various parts of the battlefield to depict combat and death, as well as more or less emphatic battlefield oratory. Later, the play again cuts cinematically from Tyre, where over a period of days or weeks Belcar recovers from his wounds with Méliane, to

Sidon, where the elderly Zorote lectures his wife on fidelity and Léonte meets her—at a ball given in his honor and presented onstage—and seduces her before dying onstage in a street battle. Comic scenes, like those involving the essentially farcical Zorote, mix freely with those depicting the wise Sidonian king's aspirations to peace or Belcar and Méliane's stolen kisses.

Even in the 1608 version, although Cassandre's suicide and Méliane's execution are described by messengers, the Tyrian king and his courtier offer a double murder onstage. Enraged because Belcar does not love her, Cassandre cries out, "Que feray-je? où courray-je? où suis-je? ardente rage!/O cheveux sans valeur, infortuné visage!" ["What will I do? Where will I run to? Where am I? Burning rage!/O worthless hair, unfortunate visage!"]. As she tears her hair and face onstage, a courtier cries out:

> Comment! que faites-vous? qu'ont fait ces fils deliez
> Mieux dorés que l'or fin qui pendent jusqu'aux pieds?
> Pourquoy les brisez vous? et ces pommes jumelles
> Pourquoy les plombez vous de froisseures cruelles
> D'où vient cest oeil hagard, et ce front esperdu
> De coups d'ongles saigneux?

[What! What are you doing? What has this fallen hair, more golden than pure gold and hanging to your feet, done to you? Why do you tear at it? And these twin apples, why do you delve into them with cruel wounds? Why this haggard eye and this forehead destroyed by bleeding nail wounds?] (p. 107).

Living in the consensus Renaissance and baroque world of incarnation and personification of the forces of nature, the Sidonian king emphatically condemns his opposite number, of whom, he says:

> Les Dieux . . . ont horreur, les Astres pour vengeance
> Ne dardent plus sur nous nulle bonne influence,
> Les champs, les ruisseaux, l'air, l'Atlantide, sont las
> De porter, de couler, d'ouïr, de mener bas,
> Les charoignes, le sang, les hurlemens, les ombres,
> Des mortels succombants au fort des encombres . . .

[The gods . . . have horror, and for revenge the stars no longer shine down any good influence upon us; the fields, the brooks, the Atlantian air are too weak to carry, to run, to hear, to carry down the dead, the blood, the screams and the shadows of mortals who succumb beneath her ruins . . .] (p. 123).

These and numerous other emphatic speeches in the style of Hardy or Corneille's *Clitandre*, abundant in the 1608 version, reappear with minor modifications in the 1628 edition (pp. 176, 236, 288). At the same time, the later play's 1,700 additional lines add new elements of horror, incarnation, and emphatic style (see pp. 192, 229, etc.). Moreover, the increased number of *péripéties* and the frequent intercutting of the 1628 text multiply contrasts, metamorphoses, and surprises. The second text offers a new scene in which Belcar saves Méliane from the torturer and emphatically offers to take her place. The ending of the tragicomedy, in which the Tyrian king relents instead of insisting on torture and death and in which a happy marriage unites the two crowns, might well be taken as a relatively more tranquil, relatively more positive and organic acceptance of life.

Both versions of *Tyr et Sidon,* therefore, pay homage to the consensus categories and definitions of baroque theatrical style. The 1628 version, moreover, carries out in many respects the "baroque theater" doctrine of François Ogier's remarkable preface, first published in the 1628 edition of Schélandre's play. Curiously, if any comparison is to be made between the two versions, the 1628 version is more classical in terms of dramatic conflict, dramatic "illusion," and psychological motivation, but at the same time more baroque in terms of the categories of Imbrie Buffum, for example. Actually, *Tyr et Sidon* is also thus part of that theatrical movement, actually more or less contemporary with the development of the rules of classicism, which ostentatiously ignored and departed from any such rules in favor of an aesthetic of multiplicity, license, and baroque horror and theatricality. More classical than Montchrestien or Hardy, the 1628 work is also a "more baroque" play suggestive of Corneille's *Clitandre* and *Médée* or Rotrou's *Bague de l'oubli* or *Venceslas.*

Any such later baroque style, flourishing alongside the first masterpieces of classicism, cannot therefore be said to determine chronologically any period of French literature, a problem which has occupied the attention of such critics as Marcel Raymond, Buffum, and Jean Rousset, among others. In his *Littérature de l'âge baroque en France,* Rousset writes with some perplexity that classicism is not the opposite of baroque, but stands in some more complex relation to it. What that relation may be is elucidated by further study of Schélandre's *Tyr et Sidon* in terms of the epistemological criteria previously applied to Ronsard, Montaigne, *L'Astrée,* and others in earlier chapters.

IF BAROQUE ELEMENTS contribute to the dramatic interest of both versions, both texts also offer an epistemological dimension expressed through the vocabulary of both resemblance and classification. In slightly different terms both contain pre-Cartesian and Cartesian, old paradigm and new paradigm, elements. Like Montaigne and Charron, the Tyrian king of the second text exhibits a typically baroque mental state as he awaits the outcome of the battle:

> Dieux! que j'ay de pensers l'un l'autre seduisans!
> De mouvements d'esprit l'un l'autre destruisans!
> Combien d'impatience agite mon attente!
> Et que mon esperance est douteuse et flottante!

[Gods! How many thoughts have I, seducing one another! How many mental movements destroying one another! How agitated is my vigil, and how doubtful and floating my hope!] (p. 182).

Both versions depict love as the enemy of reason. In both versions the Tyrian king angrily rejects anyone who may undertake to "me philosopher" (p. 92; cf. p. 274–75). In both versions the nurse Eurydice reasons both progressively or Cartesianly and also analogically, in the tradition of the Renaissance tragedy, that

> Comme le trop de bois estouffe un petit feu,
> S'il est mis sagement le grossit peu à peu,
> Ainsi de nos faveurs dont ils bruslent d'envie,
> Trop esteint leur amour peu l'entretient en vie,
>
> . . . .
>
> ... Comme en la grande masse
> D'un antique palais, une seule crevasse
> Croissant avec le temps le faict tendre au declin,
> Fait bresche irreparable et le renverse en fin:
> De semblable progrés la poursuite soigneuse
> Seduit la chair fragile ...

[Just as too much wood smothers a small fire, but if added carefully makes it grow little by little, thus it is with our favors, which they burn to receive; too much extinguishes their love, a little keeps it alive.... Just as in the great mass of an ancient palace a single

74

crack, growing with time makes it slowly decay, makes an irreparable opening and pulls it down in the end, with similar progress careful pursuit woos fragile flesh . . .] (p. 63; cf. p. 246).

References to the stars in both versions owe much more to the old science than to the new. In both texts Belcar explains to Méliane that "comme de nature au ciel le feu s'envole,/Le pesant tend à terre, et l'aimant vers le pole,/L'amoureux ne fait rien qui ne tire à ce point" ["just as nature makes fire fly into the sky, the weighty fall to earth, and the magnet toward the pole, so the lover does nothing which does not tend toward this end"] (p. 68; cf. p. 272). And in a passage first published in the second version, a personage declares:

> L'esclat de vostre front, second astre de Mars,
> Agira sans harangue au coeur de vos soldars:
> Astre qui luit sur eux en riante planette,
> Comme sur l'adversaire en sinistre comette:
> Astre à son relever influant leur valeur,
> Ainsi que son eclipse a causé leur malheur . . .

[The brilliance of your forehead, second star of Mars, will act without any speech on the heart of your soldiers: a star which shines on them as a smiling planet as it does on the enemy as a sinister comet; star influencing their valor as it rises, just as its eclipse caused their misfortune . . .] (pp. 177–78).

Both the 1608 and 1628 versions, moreover, add to the epistemology of resemblance the epistemology of representation. As in *L'Astrée* and indeed Girard Thibault, an extensive body of commentary discusses the personages' actions in terms of metaphors of law and justice. In particular, after the murder of Léonte, the Sidonian king and his lieutenant debate possible reactions to the news in Tyre, in a stichomythia based squarely on the legal problems involved:

> ARISTARQUE
> Il peut pour s'alleger son prisonnier occir.
>
> BALORTE
> Sçauroit-il contre vous un pretexte produire?
>
> ARISTARQUE
> Le pretexte ne manque à qui tasche de nuire.
> · · · · · ·

BALORTE
Le ciel n'est-il tesmoin de vostre integrité?

ARISTARQUE
Souvent perit le juste et ne l'a merité.

[ARISTARQUE
He may, to console himself, execute his prisoner.

BALORTE
Can he produce some pretext against you?

ARISTARQUE
The pretext is never lacking for whoever tries to do harm.

. . . .

BALORTE
Are not the heavens witness to your integrity?

ARISTARQUE
Often the just perish and have not merited it.]

The dialogue ends with an appeal by Aristarque to that

Juge sans appel dont les justes arrests
Traittent chacun vivant à l'egale de ses faits:
Si depuis mon Printemps, deslors que ton Astree
Du vray temple d'honneur me descouvrit l'entree
J'ay pratiqué ses loix . . .

[Ultimate judge whose just decrees treat each living person equally
to his deeds; if since my Spring, when your Astrea revealed to me
the entrance to the true temple of honor, I have practiced her
laws. . . .]. (pp. 125–26; cf. pp. 235–36).

Belcar himself unconsciously echoes his father's preoccupations when,
as he stands accused by transference before the Tyrian king, he insists
peremptorily: "Fondez vostre soupçon de preuve suffisante" ["Found
your suspicions on sufficient proof"] (p. 93; cf. p. 274).

When the Tyrian king convenes his judges to legalize the execution
of Méliane, the judges answer with considerable courage, given their
monarch's irascible habits. Their response is a defense of equity and
impersonality in justice:

Ou d'un mot absolu, Sire, il faut envoyer
La pucelle au supplice et sans nous employer,

Ou si (comme en tout temps) l'equité vous commande,
Exposez les raisons de vostre ire si grande
Lors nous mettrons bien tost les bonnes en alloy,
Preuvant l'or de justice au creuzet de la loy;
Nos coups sont importants, ne faut à la legere
(Moins la fille d'un Roy) convaincre une bergere.

[Either with an absolute word, Sire, you must send the virgin to be tortured, without recourse to us, or if (as is always the case) equity commands you, set forth the reasons for your very great anger, and then we will put the good ones to the test, assaying the gold of justice in the crucible of the law; our acts are important, we must not lightly (even less so for the daughter of a king) convict a shepherdess.]

Although anxious to get on with the execution, the coleric Tiribaze himself protests that

Or bien je ne prens point pour regle mon courroux,
Comme un simple accusant je parle devant vous,
Non comme un souverain, comme un pere en furie
Qui a pour son enfant et de mort et de vie
L'impunissable choix, je devest tout pouvoir
Fors le commun credit qu'un tesmoin doit avoir . . .

[Now indeed I do not take as my rule my anger, I speak before you as a simple accuser, not as a sovereign, nor as a furious father who has over his child the unpunishable right of life and death; I divest myself of all such power, except the common credibility which a witness should have . . .]. (pp. 135–36; cf. p. 302; see also pp. 60, 145–46, 225, 242, 310).

IN BOTH TEXTS, the movement from relatively analogical modes of thought toward relatively impersonal and, so to speak, "objective" ones is expressed in the possibly unsound and unwarranted application of quantitative methods to moral problems. In particular, the personages of *Tyr et Sidon* apply a notion already suggested in *L'Astrée* before it became a cornerstone of the Cartesian method, that of organizing problems in terms of progressions of difficulty, or complexity, or value. In a passage already quoted above, Cassandre's nurse extolls the virtues of slow progression in sexual and sentimental favors (p. 74). Méliane makes a similar point to Belcar when she explains that extreme measures in love and marriage are to be tried only as a last resort:

... comme un medecin du premier coup n'emplaye [*sic*]
La scie et le rasoir sur la nouvelle playe,
Ains esprouve à l'abord ses remedes plus lents
S'il les voit inutils use des violents:
Ainsi, tout hazarder n'est rien qu'une folie
A qui peut autrement. Belcar je te supplie,
Donte mon cher amy ce dereiglé desir.

[just as a doctor does not use at first try the saw and the razor on a
new wound, but tries out first his slower remedies, and if he sees
they do not work uses the more violent ones; thus, to chance everything is nothing but folly for whoever can do otherwise. Belcar,
I beg you, master this unregulated desire.] (p. 68; cf. p. 272 and
pp. 64, 124, 246).

To a much greater extent in the second version than in the first, sentimental problems and values are expressed in terms of money, so that in
the 1628 edition money and financial value — like legal preoccupations —
become a recurring metaphor. In both versions, fifteen to thirty-five
years before a similar scene in Corneille's *Le Menteur,* a moment of
amorous *badinage* between Belcar and Méliane takes the form of a
discussion about whether gratuitous gifts are better than well-merited
ones. Such discussion, moreover, is summarized elsewhere in the play
by the sentence, "Il n'est rien mieux acquis qu'une chose donnée"
["There is nothing better gotten than something given"] (p. 144; 1608
text). In a remark without apparent equivalent in the early edition,
however, a soldier-turned-assassin complains at length about the poor
economic status of his profession:

Vous croiriez à leur dire, et mesme des plus chiches,
Qu'au sortir du combat ils nous feront tous riches,
Qu'en peres des soldats partageans le butin,
Nous [*sic*] piques nous seront des aulnes à satin:
Mais si tost qu'ils ont veu l'occasion passee,
La liberalité leur sort de la pensee ...

[To hear them talk you would believe, and even the most stingy,
that at the issue of combat they will make us all rich, that like
fathers of the soldier dividing the booty, they will make our spears
into bolts of satin; but as soon as they see the occasion is past,
liberality goes out of their thoughts ...] (p. 224; cf. p. 231).

Also in the second version, the Tyrian king is pleased to state that his ancestors' policies have brought new prosperity to his kingdom. Thus Hiram, moved by considerations which might seem, somehow, unaristo-cratic, nevertheless:

> Mesla si dextrement les honneurs aux profits
> Qu'ils mirent en leur temps dans l'enclos de leurs terres
> L'or au prix de l'argent, l'argent au prix des pierres . . .

[Mixed so dextrously honors with profits, that in their time they put into the confines of their lands gold at the price of silver, silver at the price of stones . . .] (p. 182; cf. p. 201).

Finally, in the second version the bourgeois husband Zorote counsels his wife Philoline to spend her time "Tantost à calculer les biens par nous acquis,/Tantost du fin alloy démesler la monnoye . . . " ["Now calculating the goods we have acquired, now sorting good coins from counterfeit . . . "] (p. 188). Elsewhere, as he returns home drunk from a night on the town, Zorote ruminates to himself in monologue that "Ni le pain ni le vin ne m'ont pas semblé cher,/Mais on ma bien vendu ce que j'ay pris de chair" ["Neither bread nor wine seemed dear to me, but I was oversold on what I took of flesh"] (p. 218). Awaiting the results of his assassination plot, Zorote reflects, in terms appropriate to a bour-geois husband, perhaps, but comically inappropriate for an avenging killer:

> Je crains d'estre pipé par mes tireurs de laine:
> Car j'ay mis mon argent sur la foy d'un soldat,
> Sans pleige ni tesmoin de nostre concordat.
> Combien le jugement se dissipe et se change
> En un pauvre jaloux . . .

[I fear being tricked by my cutpurses, for I advanced my money on the word of a soldier, without any pledge or witness to our agreement. How judgment is dissipated and changed in an old jealous man . . .] (p. 260).

The 1628 version of *Tyr et Sidon* also presents for the first time a curi-ously Léonide-like discussion of the baroque-classical epistemological problem of identity. With something like the enthusiasm of someone who has discovered a new method and hopes to use it for problems for which it may (or may not) later prove appropriate, the nurse Almodice proposes to satisfy the unhappy Cassandre by substituting her for Méliane in the boat that will take Belcar—and Cassandre—to safety.

Part of the justification for this ill-fated escape plan is the nurse's bizarre idea that such a substitution would perhaps not be very important. She reasons curiously that the two sisters are, in their essential characteristics, almost identical. Belcar may not even notice the difference:

> Mesme en l'effet peut-estre il n'y pensera point,
> En pareille charnure et pareil embonpoint,
> Et l'une et l'autre pièce ont un egale usage;
> Hors la diversité qui paroist au visage
> (Où l'oeil n'est abusé que par l'eschantillon),
> Tout est d'un mesme drap prest à mettre au foulon.

[Indeed, when it happens, perhaps he will not even think about it; with similar flesh and similar figure, one and the other are used for the same thing; except for the diversity which appears in the face (in which the eye is merely tricked by the display), everything is the same whole cloth ready to be sized.] (p. 268).

If the nurse's notion of love is simplistic, other views of love in *Tyr et Sidon* are more significant. Schélandre's text returns to another problem already enunciated in *L'Astrée,* that curious anomaly of seventeenth-century French literature, the concept of *amour-estime* and its corollary, the possible conflict of love and duty. Touched upon in Léonide's argument as presented in a previous chapter, these issues are discussed extensively elsewhere in *L'Astrée.* Both versions of *Tyr et Sidon* evoke conflicts of love and duty in terms reminiscent of *L'Astrée* and suggestive of the Cornelian theater. In the 1608 text, torn between love for Belcar and grief for her murdered brother Léonte, Méliane delivers one of those monologues that Corneille was later to say were much in vogue in the decades preceding *Le Cid:*

> Plaindray-je le destin de mon unique frere
> Autrefois mon support, aujourd'hui ma misere?
> Voila de mon Belcar le tourment preparé,
> Qui seul Roy de mon coeur veut estre preferé:
> Et si de mon plus cher l'encombre je lamente,
> Le sang m'est un remords la pudeur me tourmente,
> Tant pour mettre en oubly le malheur fraternel,
> Que pour couver en l'ame un amour criminel:
> Il faut ô desespoir! que je sois declaree
> Ou desloyale amante ou soeur desnaturee:

> Et bien que les deux points de ma calamité
> Soyent d'une mesme source et mesme qualité,
> Le premier des meschefs fait que ma plainte n'ose
> Eventer le second dont il est seule cause,
> Et faut (si je le puis) ô double creve-coeur?
> Tesmoigner un desir de quoy j'ay plus de peur.

[Shall I pity the destiny of my only brother, in other times my sustenance, today my misery? Thus is the torment prepared for my own Belcar, who wants to be preferred as the sole king of my heart; and if I lament the pain of my dearest, my blood is my remorse, and shame torments me, as much if I put away my brother's misfortune as if I keep warm in my heart a criminal love. O despair! I must be declared either a disloyal lover or a perverted sister; and although the two points of my calamity have a single source and a single quality, the first of these misfortunes is such that I dare not mourn the second of which it is the sole cause, and I must (if I can do it), o double misfortune, espouse a desire which I supremely fear.] (p. 97).

Méliane's lament returns in the 1628 edition, with very striking modifications in the direction of a more quantitative approach to this heroine's moral dilemma:

> Que diray-je à ce coup? lequel de mes malheurs
> Aura le premier rang dans le cours de mes pleurs?
> Dois-je voüer ma plainte à mon unique frere,
> Autre-fois mon support, aujourd'huy ma misere?

[What shall I say of this blow? Which of my misfortunes will have the first rank in the course of my weeping? Shall I dedicate my complaint to my only brother, once my sustenance, today my misery?] (p. 276).

Méliane concludes in both versions that she alone loves Belcar and can and should come to his aid, whereas in Léonte's case "un bel oeil a regné/ De pouvoir souverain sur ton coeur esloigné" ["a beautiful eye has reigned with sovereign power over your far-off heart"] (pp. 97–98; cf. variant p. 277). However, the 1628 edition adds, in a more pertinent, specific, and hierarchical response to the moral questions addressed, that

> Et moy qui suis ta soeur, qui ne te cede point
> En ceste passion qui deux ames conjoint,

Permets en t'imitant, que le deuil je prefere
D'un amant que je pers à la perte d'un frere . . .

[And I who am your sister, who in no way cede to you in that passion which joins two souls together, permit me, in imitating you, to prefer the mourning of a lover to the loss of a brother . . .] (p. 277).

In quasi-structuralist—but also, more specifically, Cartesian fashion—Méliane identifies salient factors, constructs a plane in which those factors are comparable on a scale of value, arranges them on that scale, and finally chooses the higher ranking interest against the lesser. Such a solution is one more allusion to the double character of the play, as it depicts the parallel misfortunes of two cities, two kings, two princes, two rival sisters, and two approaches to the understanding of the world.

Both these approaches are represented in both versions of the play. In the earlier version, however, retaining a relatively more absolute, emblematic character, the interests of Tyre, Sidon, Aristarque, Tiribaze, Belcar, Léonte, Méliane, and Cassandre remain essentially unresolved. Like those of so many sublime heroes and heroines of the sixteenth-century theater, their sufferings are exemplary and their deaths presumably transcendent. In the later version, however, the conflicts of the two cities and the various other interests are relatively quantified; they are also constructively mediated. Although the prosperity of Tyre is perhaps opposed to that of Sidon, the benefits of peace opposed to the spoils of war, the joys of familial and heroic love perhaps logically incompatible, it is the very course of events, the decision of various personages simply to abandon logic and relent which, in the end, permits a happy resolution of an otherwise ineluctable conflict. Rather than a result of the play of profound and elemental forces, the denouement of Schélandre's 1628 play is essentially a result of the play of narrative contingency—or of an interplay of emblem and reason, metaphor and classification toward some kind of mediated outcome. In the 1628 version, when Pharnabaze finally pardons the two young lovers and assures the union of the two crowns, Méliane's and Belcar's love, elsewhere described as a passion of harmonious nature, or the fruit of esteem, becomes a phenomenon of overwhelming force, of victorious contingency. As Méliane herself says at the conclusion:

. . . mon amour invincible
Rompt tout autre devoir et m'y rend insensible.

Il n'est aucune loy, soit de nature ou d'art,
Que ceste passion ne rejette à l'escart.

[. . . my invincible love breaks and renders me insensitive to every other duty. There is no law, whether of nature or of art, that this passion does not cast aside] (p. 321).

The end result of this contingent event is the union of two crowns and two cities. And on the epistemological level, the discussion by which this conclusion is achieved in the 1628 edition is further evidence that any epistemic transformation as posited by Foucault did not occur suddenly in a brief period, say from 1605 to 1615. Neither is any such transformation the exclusive property of a baroque aesthetic or a classicist aesthetic—the later *Tyr et Sidon* contains passages suggestive both of the baroque and the classicist masterpieces of the 1630s and 1640s. Instead, as Kuhn might suggest, Schélandre's play is simply one of a great many artifacts of the working out of a new mode of understanding of the world. Such artifacts are so numerous in the middle decades of the seventeenth century—and their implications so various—that they are treated in Chapter 7 on the recurring seventeenth-century theme, or classeme, of love and duty.

NOTES

1. Montchrestien, *Hector,* in J. Schérer, ed., *Théâtre du XVIIᵉ siècle* (Paris: Pléiade, 1975), p. 3.

2. T. J. Reiss, *Toward Dramatic Illusion* (New Haven: Yale University Press, 1971).

3. Schélandre, *Tyr et Sidon* (Paris: Nizet, 1975), pp. 53, 166. Citations are henceforth given in the text.

CHAPTER 7

Two Reflections on Love and Duty:
Bradamante and *Le Cid*

HONORÉ D'URFÉ WRITES in *L'Astrée* that "Il est impossible d'aimer ce que l'on n'estime pas" ["it is impossible to love what one does not esteem"]. He writes also that there is "rien qui touche plus vivement, qu'opposer l'honneur à l'amour..." ["Nothing touches more vividly than to oppose honor to love..."]. These two related subjects are discussed extensively elsewhere in *L'Astrée,* as a preceding chapter suggests. And as Chapter 6 shows, they are also discussed extensively in Schélandre's *Tyr et Sidon*. Traditionally, literary history associates the curious seventeenth-century anomalies of *amour-estime* and related conflicts of love and duty with the theater of Corneille and most especially with his very great success of the 1636–37 season, *Le Cid.*[1]

Corneille's tragicomedy is itself often compared with the first French "tragecomedie," Garnier's *Bradamante* of 1582. In his preface to a modern edition of *Bradamante,* Marcel Hervier writes that "Par la liberté et la variété du ton, par une inspiration plus française qu'italienne... par la vivacité des sentiments qui dans des situations toutes romanesques gardent du naturel et de la simplicité, en dépit des maladresses techniques et de longueurs, elle a une fraîcheur poétique qu'on ne retrouvera que dans *Le Cid,* autre sujet du moyen âge" ["by its liberty and variety of tone, by a more French than Italian inspiration... by the vivacity of sentiments which, in highly Romanesque situations, remain simple and natural, in spite of technical faults and tedious passages, it has a poetic freshness which will not be found again until *Le Cid,* another medieval subject"]. Similarly, in a recent article on "The Place of Garnier's *Bradamante* in Dramatic History," Donald Stone, Jr., writes that for *Bradamante* to be transformed into *Le Cid,* "French literature has to pass through préciosité, a gradual discrediting of humanism and a long exposure to and treatment of the theme of love."[2]

In *Bradamante,* it develops that whoever wants to marry the heroine Bradamante must first defeat her in single combat, an art at which she is highly accomplished. Bradamante has issued this challenge because she does not want to marry her eminent suitor, Léon, but instead the knight Roger. She believes that only Roger is capable of defeating her. However, she is unaware that Roger is obligated to Léon and feels he must fulfill his obligation by fighting Bradamante on Léon's rather than his own behalf. Roger describes his moral and sentimental dilemma in a striking monologue:

> Me voici desguisé, mais c'est pour me tromper.
> Je porte un coutelas, mais c'est pour m'en frapper.
> J'entre dans le combat pour me vaincre moymesme.
> Le prix de ma victoire est ma despouille mesme.
> Qui veit onc tel malheur? Leon triomphera
> De Roger, et Roger sa victoire acquerra:
> Je suis ore Leon et Roger tout ensemble.
>   Chose estrange! un contraire au contraire s'assemble.
> Qu'il m'eust bien mieux valu souffrir l'affliction
> D'où Leon me tira, que cette passion!
> Helas je suis entré d'un mal en un martyre!
> De tous aspres tourmens mon tourment est le pire.
> A mon sort les Enfers de semblables n'ont rien!
> Ils ont divers tourmens, mais moy je suis le mien,
> Moymesme me punis, moymesme me bourrelle;
> Je suis mon punisseur et ma peine cruelle;
> Je me suis ma Mégère et mes noirs coulevreaux,
> Mes cordes et mes fers, mes fouets et mes flambeaux.
> O piteux infortune! Ay-je esté si mal sage,
> Si privé de bon sens que jurer mon dommage?
> Que promettre à Leon de luy livrer mon coeur,
> Et d'estre de moymesme à son profit vaincueur?
> Encor si à moy seul je faisois cet outrage.
> Mais Bradamante, hélas! le souffre davantage.
> Il faut n'en faire rien. Mais quoy? tu l'as promis.
> C'est tout un; ne m'en chaut, il n'estoit pas permis.
> Si ma promesse estoit de faire à Dieu la guerre,
> A mon pere, à ma race, à ma natale terre,
> La devroy-je tenir? non, non, seroit mal fait.
> De promesse mechante est tres mechant l'effet.
> Voire, mais tu luy es attenu de ta vie.
> Las! de ma vie, ouy bien, mais non pas de m'amie.
> Il est venu de Grece en France sous ta foy.
> S'est offert au combat se faisant fort de toy;

Tout ton honneur y pend, il n'est pas raisonnable
De luy faulser promesse estant son redevable.
Allons donc, de par Dieu, puis que j'y suis tenu.

[Here I am disguised, but it is to trick myself. I carry a cutlass, but it is to strike myself. I enter into combat to conquer myself. The prize of my victory is my own destitution. Who ever saw such bad fortune? Léon will triumph over Roger, and Roger will acquire his victory: Henceforth I am Léon and Roger all together.

Strange thing! A contrary to its opposite is assembled. It would have been much better form to suffer the affliction from which Léon saved me than this passion! Alas, I have gone from evil to martyrdom! Of all the bitter torments, mine is the worst. Hell has nothing similar to my destiny. They have divers torments, but I am my own torment, I punish myself, I am my own executioner; I am my punisher and my cruel punishment; I am the Megaera and my black vipers, my ropes and my irons, my whips and my torches. O piteous misfortune! Have I been so unwise, so deprived of good sense as to swear my own hurt? To promise to Léon to give him my heart and to be myself to his own profit the conqueror? Not so bad if I were doing this to myself alone, but Bradamante, alas, suffers from it even more. I should do nothing. But how? You promised. It's all the same; it makes no difference; it was not permitted. If my promise were to make war on God, on my father, on my race, or on my homeland, should I keep it? No, no, that would be evil. An evil promise has an evil effect. All right, but you owe him your life. Alas, my life, no doubt, but not my sweetheart. He came from Greece to France on your assurances. He offered himself for combat because he was sure of your support; all his honor depends on it, and it is not reasonable to break a promise when I am in his debt. All right, let's go, by God, since there is no way out.]

As is well known, in *Le Cid* the young hero Don Rodrique is obliged by his father to save the family honor by fighting a duel with the father of his beloved fiancée, Doña Chimène. He ponders his love and his moral duty in a famous monologue quite similar to that of Roger in the earlier play:

Percé jusques au fond du coeur
D'une atteinte imprévue aussi bien que mortelle,
Misérable vengeur d'une juste querelle,
Et malheureux objet d'une injuste rigueur,

Je demeure immobile, et mon âme abattue
Cède au coup qui me tue.
Si près de voir mon feu récompensé,
O Dieu, l'étrange peine!
En cet affront mon père est l'offensé,
Et l'offenseur le père de Chimène!

Que je sens de rudes combats!
Contre mon propre honneur mon amour s'intéresse
Il faut venger un père, et perdre une maîtresse:
L'un m'anime le coeur, l'autre retient mon bras.
Réduit au triste choix ou de trahir ma flamme,
Ou de vivre en infâme,
Des deux côtés mon mal est infini.
O Dieu, l'étrange peine!
Faut-il laisser un affront impuni?
Faut-il punir le père de Chimène?

Père, maîtresse, honneur, amour,
Noble et dure contrainte, aimable tyrannie,
Tous mes plaisirs sont morts, ou ma gloire ternie.
L'un me rend malheureux, l'autre indigne du jour.
Cher et cruel espoir d'une âme généreuse,
Mais ensemble amoureuse,
Digne ennemi de mon plus grand bonheur,
Fer qui causes ma peine,
M'es-tu donné pour venger mon honneur?
M'es-tu donné pour perdre ma Chimène?

Il vaut mieux courir au trépas.
Je dois à ma maîtresse aussi bien qu'à mon père:
J'attire en me vengeant sa haine et sa colère;
J'attire ses mépris en ne me vengeant pas.
A mon plus doux espoir l'un me rend infidèle,
Et l'autre indigne d'elle.
Mon mal augmente à le vouloir guérir;
Tout redouble ma peine.
Allons, mon âme; et puisqu'il faut mourir,
Mourons du moins sans offenser Chimène.

Mourir sans tirer ma raison!
Rechercher un trépas si mortel à ma gloire!
Endurer que l'Espagne impute à ma mémoire
D'avoir mal soutenu l'honneur de ma maison!

Respecter un amour dont mon âme égarée
   Voit la perte assurée!
N'écoutons plus ce penser suborneur,
   Qui ne sert qu'à ma peine.
Allons, mon bras, sauvons du moins l'honneur,
Puisqu'après tout il faut perdre Chimène.

      Oui, mon esprit s'était déçu.
Je dois tout à mon père avant qu'à ma maîtresse:
Que je meure au combat, ou meure de tristesse,
Je rendrai mon sang pur comme je l'ai reçu.
Je m'accuse déjà de trop de négligence:
      Courons à la vengeance;
   Et tout honteux d'avoir tant balancé,
      Ne soyons plus en peine,
Puisqu'aujourd'hui mon père est l'offensé,
Si l'offenseur est père de Chimène.

[Pierced to the bottom of my heart by a wound as unexpected as it is mortal, miserable avenger of a just quarrel, and unfortunate object of an unjust rigor, I remain immobile, and my beaten-down soul gives way to the blow which kills me. So near to seeing my flame rewarded, oh, God, what strange punishment! In this affront my father is the offended, and the offender the father of Chimène!

What rude conflict I feel! Against my own honor my love takes up the cause. I must avenge a father, and lose a mistress; one arouses my heart, the other holds back my hand. Reduced to the sad choice of betraying my flame, or living in infamy, on both sides my pain is infinite. Oh, God, what strange punishment! Must I leave an affront unpunished? Must I destroy the father of Chimène?

Father, mistress, honor, love, noble and hard constraint, lovable tyranny, all my pleasures are dead, or my honor tarnished. One makes me unhappy, the other unworthy of life. Dear and cruel hope of a noble but also loving soul, worthy enemy of my greatest happiness, blade which is causing my difficulty, were you given to me to avenge my honor? Were you given to me to lose me my Chimène?

It is better to seek death. I owe to my mistress as well as to my father. In avenging myself I inspire her hatred and her anger. But I inspire her scorn if I am not avenged. To my sweetest hope one renders me faithful, and to the other unworthy of her. My ill grows greater if I try to cure it. Everything redoubles my pain. Let us go, my soul, and since I must die, let me die at least without offending Chimène.

But die without receiving satisfaction! Seek a death so fatal for my reputation! Endure that Spain impute to my memory that I have badly supported the honor of my house! Respect a love of which my deranged mind can clearly see the loss! Let us not listen to this treacherous thought, which serves only my pain, let us go, my arm, let us at least save honor, since in any case I must lose Chimène.

Yes, my mind had deceived itself. I owe everything to my father before my mistress. Whether I die in combat or die of distress, I will shed my blood as pure as I received it. I accuse myself already of too much negligence. Let us run to vengeance: and all ashamed to have reflected so long, let us no longer worry, since today my father is the one offended, even though the offender is the father of Chimène].[3]

These very long passages require little commentary. The principles applied to Hylas's and Tyrcis's debate, on the one hand, and to Léonide's judgment, on the other, are applicable here. The first text, as it speaks of "un contraire" linked to a "contraire," bases itself clearly on an epistemology of contraries and similars—that is, on something like an *épistémè* of resemblance. Roger, at the conclusion of his monologue, simply chooses between opposing loyalties. In the second text, however, Rodrigue confronts more complex dilemmas and considers his alternatives in a different manner. Where Roger speaks of two opposing inclinations, Rodrigue, as the most traditional analysis suggests, opposes love and honor, love and esteem. And where Roger speaks of victory, defeat, punishment, and suffering, Rodrigue adopts a clearly juridical vocabulary and frame of reference. To use for a moment the terminology of present-day game theory—an approach to which the first text clearly does not lend itself—Rodrigue constructs a matrix, a game matrix, of alternative possibilities. The young hero's analysis reveals that his game has strategies that are losing ones, no matter what the course of events. It reveals further that, in the terminology of the game theoretician, his game possesses a dominant strategy—that is, an optimum strategy promising maximum benefit to Rodrigue as player, whatever the reactions of the other players. In other words, Rodrigue is able to classify and arrange in a hierarchy of value his various alternatives, choosing finally the most favorable. Analyzed in these terms, his monologue becomes, like Léonide's judgment, a representation and a mathematization of its subject. It chooses action which—just as the most traditional literary history suggests—conserves some of the benefits of both duty and love.

As THE SUBTITLES of "tragecomédie" and "tragi-comédie" suggest, both plays have positive endings. In *Bradamante* little more than elucidation is required. Sometime between the end of act 4 and the beginning of act 5, Léon—who was quite simply unaware of Roger's feelings for the heroine—seeks out Roger and learns the truth. Act 5 opens *in medias res* as Léon asks, "Mon frere, et pourquoy ne me l'avies-vous dit?" ["my brother, why didn't you tell me?"]. Now well informed, Léon simply and generously cedes Bradamante to his rival: "Je ne veux pas mon aise avoir par le trespas/Du meilleur chevalier qui se trouve icy bas" ["I don't want to gain my happiness by the death of the best knight to be found here below"]. Léon chooses between alternatives, prefers one good to another, but without the kind of reasoning displayed by Rodrigue: "combien que je l'aime autant que mon coeur mesme," he declares, "Plus qu'elle toutefois vostre vaillance j'aime./Ayez-la pour espouse . . . " ["even though I love her as much as my own heart itself, nevertheless I love your valiance more. Take her as your wife . . . "]. The rest of act 5 simply tidies up the situation, and in an otherwise unmotivated appearance the sorceress Mélisse observes that the heavens work in mysterious ways, that Roger and Bradamante's future will be illustrious, and that, in an example of Foucaldian emulation, "Tout chacun en est aise, et je crois fermement/Que l'air, l'onde et la terre en ont contentement" ["Everyone rejoices, and I firmly believe the air, the waters, and the earth rejoice in it"].[4]

The resolution of dramatic conflict in *Le Cid* is, of course, more complex. As suggested earlier, the later play deals not only with divided loyalties but also with oppositions of inclination and esteem, love and family honor, harmony and reason. Consequently, the later play also presents conflict between two different ways of seeing the world, two paradigms or perhaps two *épistémès*. The play sees these conflicting approaches, moreover, as essentially incommensurable—and hence, logically, irreconcilable. As long as the play's personages remain within the domain of sentiment, no amount of action or ratiocination can erase the count's affront to Don Diègue, nor Rodrigue's affront to Chimène. At the same time, in the domain of family honor, no amount of reasoning can justify the protagonists' real and continuing amorous emotions. As long as the speakers remain within one or the other of the two approaches, therefore, in the very suggestive terms of René Girard, no means exists to end the blood feud of warring emotions, warring interests, warring worldviews, and warring epistemologies.

Under these conditions, one might wonder how *Le Cid* succeeds in reconciling such irreconcilables, in bringing together what are, by this sort of definition, specifically incommensurable opposites. To achieve this logically impossible task, a variety of means are used; all of them at first glance are necessarily inadequate to their object. All of them are associated, moreover, with that indispensable regulatory device of Girard's *La Violence et le sacré*, royal, that is, political authority. In *Le Cid* the king—sometimes seen as weak and ineffectual—nevertheless does actually take an active and effective role in the working out of the action. First, he tries to reason with the count (through his envoy) and later with Chimène. He props up Rodrigue's reputation by praising his victory over the Moors, and he arranges a ritual duel between Rodrigue and Don Sanche, a quasi-magical approach reminiscent of such long-discredited institutions as juridical astrology. Through trickery he arranges a test of Chimène's true emotions. And finally he has recourse to the device of time—that time whose passage is said to heal all wounds. "Le temps assez souvent a rendu légitime," he declares to Chimène, "Ce qui sembloit d'abord ne se pouvoir sans crime" ["Time has often enough rendered legitimate what seemed at first inevitably a crime"]. Before the play's end, the king assures Rodrigue that all will be well and urges him simply to leave matters up to "le temps, ta vaillance, et ton roi" ["time, your valiance, and your king"].[5]

Jean Rousset writes that "on dit: ordre, mesure, raison, règle, et c'est le classicisme." He adds immediately, however, that "Le Classicisme n'est que partiellement défini par ces mots rituels." And indeed, as this analysis of *Le Cid* shows quite clearly, the much-studied phenomenon of *la raison classique* may be anything and everything but a strict observance of the rules of logic—certainly not an unbending respect for the principles of pure reason. Actually, as it presents a logically irreconcilable conflict between two paradigms or epistemologies, *Le Cid* has recourse to means that fall outside the domain of pure reason—ruse, temporizing, trickery, and personal authority, for example. It may well be that such devices are the staples of narrative fiction. Indeed, one cannot help but wonder if they do not form a repertoire that is one of a very few "eternal" constants in literary expression, one with obvious Jungian archetypal overtones.[6]

Such devices form a category of solutions used in a wide variety of seventeenth-century texts. They include all those desperate or unclassifiable or ridiculous or irrational or pararational devices of fiction which may be helpful precisely when reason fails. A reader might be tempted to call them the repertoire of "practical"—as opposed to pure and logical—reason. The sixteenth-century sometimes illogical logician Ramus called such means—or some of them—the "méthode de prudence" and devoted a long section of his *Dialectique* to them. Their presence in fiction is perhaps not surprising, since they are the mediating force which, specifically, allows the reconciliation of irreconcilable opposites, in the manner of Claude Lévi-Strauss. Yet their presence may surprise in the literature of a classical period, which systematically praises the rule of classicist reason. In the earlier texts studied in the preceding chapters, the methods of "practical" reason or of "prudence" include the abiding faith in God of Montaigne's *Apologie de Raymond Sebond,* that "dernier tour d'escrime," the "coup desesperé, auquel il faut abandonner vos armes pour faire perdre à vostre adversaire les siennes" ["the last fencing trick, the desperate ploy in which you abandon your arms to make your adversary abandon his"]. They include also the willingness to simplify problems, the hope of correctly judging the price of things in Charron and Descartes, as well as Descartes's *lumière naturelle* and provisional morality. Including but also going beyond the *épreuves* studied by narrative semiotics, they are the infinite patience and feminine disguise and tutelary mediation that permit Céladon finally to conquer the resistance of Astrée. They are also the testing and the pardon which reunite two lovers in the 1628 version of *Tyr et Sidon.* They are also the "bon pied, bon oeil" of Thibault and the gracious stepping aside of Léon in *Bradamante.*[7]

In this present-day logical—or illogical—world very little attention has been paid to the uses of illogic or paralogic or simple trickery or cunning in seventeenth-century theater and fiction. Specific cases, specific examples would necessarily be subject to exceptions, debate, objections, and more subtle analysis. In an overall view, however, it is clear that such examples do not disappear as French literature enters its period of *raison classique,* in the middle and perhaps later decades of the seventeenth century. In the earlier works of Corneille, *Clitandre* contrasts the truth of verisimilitude with the truth of contingency and resemblance. In *Clitandre* the good are saved simply because witnesses arrive in time—leaving the Pharnabaze-like king to conclude, wonderingly and emphatically, "Combien la vraisemblance a peu de verité!" ["How little truth there is in verisimilitude"]. In the *Galerie du Palais*—whose charming and picturesque and possibly baroque market scenes rehearse again the omnipresent seventeenth-century metaphor of monetary value— personages who overvalue themselves on the sentimental market are led by the play of free-market forces to better understand the *prix des choses.* In Corneille's *Illusion comique* a conflict between solid bourgeois values and the magic of the theater is resolved by the magic and trickery of Alcandre and the financial respectability of the seventeenth-century stage. In a final scene the wizard points out that "Le Theatre est un fief dont les rentes sont bonnes" ["The Theatre is a property which pays good dividends"]—a phrase with a world of meaning for both seventeenth-century social and intellectual transformations. In *Le Cid,* as has been suggested, time, valiance, and royal authority resolve logically insoluble problems; in *Horace* a wise king and the *raison d'Etat* perform a similar service, which in *Polyeucte* is performed by the grace of God. In *Cinna* the famous "clémence d'Auguste" ["Augustus's clemency"] puts an end to anti-imperial plotting better than would the strict observance of the law. Corneille's *Le Menteur* resolves a comic problem of love and duty through lies and fickle behavior. Various other mid-seventeenth-century texts resolve similar problems through the simple—but supposedly unworthy—device of the deus ex machina or comic disguises or the Mamamouchi or the like.[8]

IN GENERAL, if one recent writer on the seventeenth century has been tempted to write about its cultivation of the *absurde,* others might wish to write on the abundance of stratagems, tricks, irrational mediation, finesse, gamesmanship, and the like that abound in this supposedly rationalist age. In such tactics a Kuhnian might be tempted to see the sort of *bricolage* that characterizes attempts to repair an old paradigm or the search for a new one—or, much more likely, the more or less orderly or disorderly working out of the consequences of a newly adopted one. Similarly, a Foucaldian might well see in such "Cornelian" conflict and its more or less improvised methods of resolution the working out of the consequences of a new epistemic space. But further, a Foucaldian critic might see some of the Cornelian *bricolage,* some of the Cornelian "méthode de prudence," so widely resorted to in the masterpieces of classicism, as manifestation of one fundamental difference between any *épistémè* of resemblance and any *épistémè* of representation. According to Foucault, thinking in the mode of resemblance hopes to gain direct access to real, ultimate truth. Thinking in the mode of representation, however, recognizes that words and statements only approximate truth —recognizes that there is distance between word and thing, between truth and statement. If this is so, one might expect discussion of this imponderable distance to play some role in seventeenth-century discourse. And indeed in Corneille's *Rodogune,* as sentiments of generosity and prudence resolve a conflict of love and royal succession, the heroine speaks also of "ces je ne sais quoi qu'on ne peut expliquer" ["these *je ne sais quoi* that we cannot explain"]. Discussion of such imponderables as taste or the *art de plaire* or most especially the *je ne sais quoi* is, of course, extensive in the seventeenth century.[9]

A recurring assertion in mid-seventeenth-century discourse is that reason, after all, is not all there is to truth and understanding. Guez de Balzac writes, for example, that one should not insist on "cette exacte et rigoureuse Justice. Ne vous attachez point avec tant de scrupule à la souveraine raison: qui voudroit la contenter, et suivre ses desseins et sa regularité, seroit obligé de luy bastir un plus beau monde que cettui-ci: Il faudroit luy faire faire une nouvelle Nature des choses, et luy aller chercher des Idées au-dessus du Ciel" ["that exact and rigorous justice. Do not be so scrupulously attached to sovereign reason: whoever might wish to content her, and follow her designs and her regularity, would be obliged to build a more beautiful world than this one; one would have to make for her a new nature of things, and go to search for ideas above the sky"]. Someone might wish to study in this same light the elusive morality—or antimorality—of Molière, from the pseudo-epistemology of resemblance of the ridiculous *précieuses* to the pseudo-epistemology of classification of the ridiculous *femmes savantes.* Pascal, meanwhile, writes extensively on the opposite but in some ways symmetrical spirits of geometry and finesse—as well as of the heart which "a ses raisons que la raison ne connaît point" ["has its reasons which reason knows nothing about"]. Pascal's Jansenism and his terse assertion that "la loi était figurative" ["the Law was figurative"] rehearse again this major seventeenth-century epistemological issue. It would be impossible, of course, to do justice in these pages to the very wide variety of seventeenth-century texts which might—or might not—lend themselves to study along similar lines.[10]

However far one might wish to follow any such leaps of explanation, it is clear that the evolution toward classification, hierarchization, and epistemological *bricolage* represented by *Bradamante* and *Le Cid* and reflected more—or less—extensively in other mid-seventeenth-century French texts suggests less the struggle and final triumph of rival aesthetics or *épistémès,* nor the simply historical coexistence of differing writers and schools, than a variety of alternative responses to a single crisis in epistemology. If the baroque and mannerist traits identified with literature leading up to the first and second decades of the seventeenth century can properly be seen as signs of awareness of an epistemological malaise, then as a new epistemological dimension appears, the literature of the second and later decades of the same century may appropriately be understood as responses of opposition (preciosity), resignation (Jansenism), paradox (burlesque), or indeed assimilation and reconciliation (later baroque and classicist works) to the same crisis.

In particular, in the context of current, theoretically unsatisfying definitions of the baroque style, such a model would suggest that there are something like two baroque styles, using in part the same repertoire of images and ideas, but clearly separable in time as part of two stages of historical development in literature. In such a view, a first baroque, or baroque-and-mannerist period, reflecting growing crisis, is followed by a second baroque-and-emerging classical period reflecting varying types of assimilation of a new paradigm of epistemological—or epistemic—assumptions. In such a model the optimism, the "organic unity," and the "acceptance of life" of certain early baroque texts would continue to contrast strikingly with the doubt and disquietude of literary mannerism. Both, however, would represent the same perceived crisis in the world of Renaissance analogy. In the same way both early classicist works and such relatively controlled and circumscribed later baroque works as Corneille's *Illusion comique* and *Menteur* or Rotrou's *Saint-Genest* and other plays would appear as alternative, contemporary explorations of the same epistemological issues—the working out of two coexisting modes of thought, through an extensive repertoire of modes of practical or *bricolé* or "prudent" reason.

NOTES

1. D'Urfé, *Maximes* (Lyons: H. Lardanchet, 1913), 11; D'Urfé, *L'Astrée*, 1:72; 2: 4, 181 (?); Corneille, *Le Cid*, in *Théâtre complet* (Paris: Garnier, n.d.).

2. Garnier, *Bradamante* (Paris: Garnier, 1949), p. xvi; Donald Stone, Jr., "The Place of Garnier's *Bradamante* in Dramatic History," *AUMLA* 26 (1966), 260–71.

3. *Bradamante,* act 3, scene 5 (pp. 56–58); Corneille, *Le Cid,* act 1, scene 6.

4. *Bradamante,* act 5, scenes 1, 6 (pp. 87, 89, 108).

5. *Le Cid,* act 5, scene 7.

6. Rousset, *La Littérature de l'âge baroque en France,* pp. 242–43. Of the very extensive bibliography of the subject of classical reason, the most suggestive for the present study is perhaps R. Michéa's "Les variations de la raison au XVIIe siècle," *Revue Philosophique de la France et de l'Etranger* 126 (1938), 183–201; it was partially reprinted in Brody, ed., *French Classicism.* More recent comments on the pararational nature of classicist reason are found in Edward Bloomberg, "Etude sémantique du mot 'raison' chez Pascal," *OL* 28 (1973), 124–37; Jean-Joseph Goux, "La Logique des classiques," *Tel Q* 24 (1965), 85–91. Erica Harth, "Exorcising the Beast: Attempts at Rationality in French Classicism," *PMLA* 88 (1973), 19–24, attacks the "continued belief that French classicism flourished in an 'age of reason' " and asserts that "French classical literature betrays not the reason by which it is usually characterized, but a largely unsuccessful striving for rational control of the irrational."

7. Ramus, *Dialectique,* pp. 128–35. Ramus cites Aristotle and Quintilian as sources for the "méthode de prudence" (p. 120). Montaigne, *Essais,* p. 626. The present exposition, of course, cannot pretend to do justice to the range and complexity of "prudence" in so extensive and varied a collection of texts.

8. Corneille, *Théâtre complet* (Paris: Gallimard, n.d.) 1:144 (*Clitandre,* act 5, scene 4), p. 569 (*L'Illusion,* act 5, scene 5). For an example of more detailed analysis in this genre, see H. De Ley, "Deux érotismes, deux modes de pensée dans les *Galanteries du duc d'Ossonne*," in J. Van Baelen and David L. Rubin, eds., *La Cohérence intérieure* (Paris: J.–M. Place, 1977), pp. 61–73.

9. Corneille, *Théâtre complet,* 2: 336 (*Rodogune,* act 1, scene 5). The bibliography of *le goût,* of the *art de plaire,* and especially the *je ne sais quoi* is extensive. Along with Benedetto Croce's *Esthetics* (New York: Noonday Press, 1953), see P. Zumthor and H. Sommer, "A propos du mot 'génie'," *ZRP* 66 (1950), 170–201, and E. Köhler, "Je ne sais quoi; ein Kapitel aus der Begriffsgeschicte des Unbegreiflichen," *RJa* 6 (1953–54), p. 21–59.

10. Quoted in Charles Sutcliffe, *Guez de Balzac* (Paris: Nizet, 1959), p. 211; Pascal, *Pensées* (Paris: Delmas, 1960), pp. 163, 244.

CHAPTER 8

Two Determinations of the Normal to a Curve: Descartes and L'Hospital

THE REMARKABLE ADVANCES in mathematics during the seventeenth century owe some of their success to purely practical reason as well as to something like the mathematical equivalents of the *je ne sais quoi*. Leaving aside such advances as logarithms (in part a simply practical aid to calculation), or Desargues's projective geometry, or Pascal and Fermat's studies of probability (firmly rooted in the practicalities of gaming), a salient feature of any possible Cartesian revolution was surely Descartes's development of what is now called analytic geometry. Descartes used the latter in a celebrated problem solution in 1631 and described it more fully in his *Géométrie* of 1637. The advantages of analytic geometry have proved to be such that Descartes is sometimes described as the first truly modern mathematician, as well as the first truly modern philosopher. In part, this is because analytic geometry is thought to have been an indispensable step toward an even more far-reaching seventeenth-century mathematical revolution—part of the so-called Newtonian revolution of the last four decades of the seventeenth century—the invention of differential and integral calculus. Apparently first used by Newton in the 1660s and reinvented by Leibniz in the following decade, the methodology of calculus is habitually referred to as the single most important turning point in the development of the mathematics of the present day.

Despite apparently universal agreement on the significance of analytic geometry and calculus in modern mathematics, historians offer a variety of models for the intellectual innovation these may represent. Traditionally, historians of science have seen their task as one of carefully weighing merit and equitably dispensing credit for those innovations that have been retained by current science—the accumulative model of science history criticized by Kuhn, among others. An accumulative view lends itself readily to the notion of major discoveries and turning points contributed by certain venerable works of genius—as, for example, the Cartesian and Newtonian "revolutions" already mentioned. At the same time, it may lend itself equally well to a conscientiously developed model of gradualism, since every discovery can presumably be shown to have sprung from more or less imperfect precursors.

For example, Carl B. Boyer writes in his very suggestive *History of the Calculus and Its Conceptual Development* that calculus was indeed the invention of Newton and Leibniz, for whom a certain number of elements considered essential fell together into a coherent set. According to the same account, however, each of these essential elements can be shown to have been anticipated in one way or another by one or by several earlier mathematicians. Close reading of Newton and Leibniz suggests that these discoverers themselves varied considerably as to the theoretical underpinnings of their work, underpinnings which were improved and perhaps definitively established only by later writers. In particular, Boyer's *History of the Calculus* attributes considerable importance to a predecessor of Descartes, François Viète. A supporter of the Huguenots and a contemporary of Charron and Malherbe, Viète published in 1591 an *Artem Analyticam Isagoge* that, although presumably not entirely original itself, had the entirely practical—rather than theoretical—merit of presenting equations in clearly symbolic and general terms, using consonants to represent constants and vowels to represent unknowns. In Boyer's view Viète's innovation was "absolutely essential to the rapid progress of analytic geometry and the calculus in the following centuries, for it permitted the concepts of variability and functionality to enter into algebraic thought. The improved notation led also to methods which were so much more facile in application than the cumbrous geometrical procedures of Archimedes, of which they were modifications, that these methods were eventually recognized as forming a new analysis—the calculus."[1]

Choosing between gradualist and revolutionary views of progress in mathematics also implies considerable elasticity in chronology. Boyer's book begins with Archimedes and ends, more or less, with Cauchy, a period covering most of the history of Western civilization. Boyer speaks also of a "Century of Anticipation,"[2] the period of some ninety years between Viète and Leibniz. Taking a somewhat different point of view, however, the time between Descartes's *Géométrie* of 1637 and Newton's discoveries, apparently made sometime around 1665, is slightly under thirty years. The time between Newton and such other near-discoverers of the calculus as Hudde or Sluse or Barrow is smaller still, or perhaps nonexistent.

Under such conditions one might question whether any one specific discovery—whether Viète's notation or Sluse's or Barrow's version of pre-calculus, presumably easy to pastiche once discovered or, as the record abundantly demonstrates, possible to arrive at independently—is as important as certain shared conceptions of the object of inquiry and the methods of investigation implied by any specific text or any specific group or pair of texts. A remarkable example is provided by two texts addressing similar problems, the first from Descartes's *Géométrie* of 1637 and the second from Guillaume de l'Hospital's *Analyse des infiniment petits* of 1696.

THE CARTESIAN TEXT appears in the second book of the *Géométrie*. Descartes first interrupts a series of proofs to comment on the significance of the material he is presenting. He then gives a general method for determining the normal, that is, the line perpendicular to a given curve at a given point. Finally, he applies the general method to determine the normal to a given point on an ellipse.

> ...Et enfin pour cequi est de toutes les autres proprietés qu'on peut attribuer aux lignes courbes, elles ne dependent que de la grandeur des angles qu'elles font avec quelques autres lignes. Mais lorsqu'on peut tirer des lignes droites qui les couppent a angles droits, aux poins ou elles sont recontrées par celles avec qui elles font les angles qu'on veut mesurer, ou, ce que je prens icy pour le mesme, qui couppent leurs contingentes; la grandeur de ces angles n'est pas plus malaysée a trouver, que s'ils estoient compris entre deux lignes droites. C'est pourquoy je croyray avoir mis icy tout ce qui est requis pour les elemens des lignes courbes, lorsque j'auray generalement donné la façon de tirer des lignes droites, qui tombent a angles droits sur tels de leurs poins qu'on voudra choisir. Et j'ose dire que c'est cecy le problesme le plus utile, et le plus general non seulement que je sçache, mais mesme que j'aye jamais desiré de sçavoir en Geometrie.
>
> Soit CE la ligne courbe, et qu'il faille tirer une ligne droite par le point C, qui face avec elle des angles droits. Je suppose la chose desja faite, et que la ligne cherchée est CP, laquelle je prolonge jusques au point P, ou elle rencontre la ligne droite GA, que je suppose estre celle aux poins de laquelle on rapporte tous ceux de

la ligne CE: en sorte que faisant MA ou CB = y, et CM, ou BA = x, j'ay quelque equation, qui explique le rapport, qui est entre x et y. Puis je fais PC = s, et PA = v, ou PM = $v - y$, et a cause du triangle rectangle PMC j'ay ss, qui est le quarré de la baze esgale à $xx + vv - 2vy + yy$, qui sont les quarrés des deux costés. C'est a dire j'ay $x = \sqrt{ss - vv + 2vy - yy}$, ou bien $y = v + \sqrt{ss - xx}$, et par le moyen de cete equation, j'oste de l'autre equation qui m'explique le rapport qu'ont tous les poins de la courbe CE a ceux de la droite GA, l'une des deux quantités indeterminées x ou y. Ce qui est aysé a faire en mettant partout $\sqrt{ss - vv + 2vy - yy}$ au lieu d'x, et le quarré de cete somme au lieu d'xx, et son cube au lieu d'x^3, et ainsi des autres, si c'est x que je veuille oster; ou bien si c'est y, en mettant en son lieu $[v] + \sqrt{ss - xx}$, et le quarré, ou le cube, etc. de cete somme, au lieu d'yy, ou y^3 etc. De façon qu'il reste tousjours aprés cela une equation, en laquelle il n'y a plus qu'une seule quantité indeterminée, x, ou y.

Comme si CE est une Ellipse, et que MA soit le segment de son diametre, auquel CM soit appliquée par ordre, et qui ait r pour son costé droit, et q pour le traversant, on à [sic] par le 13 th. du I liv. d'Apollonius. $xx = ry - \dfrac{r}{q} yy$, d'on [sic] ostant xx, il reste $ss - vv + 2vy - yy = ry - \dfrac{r}{q} yy$. Ou bien,

$$yy\dfrac{+ qry - 2qvy + qvv - qss}{q - r} \text{ égal a rien.}$$

Car il est mieux en cet endroit de considerer ainsi ensemble toute la somme, que d'en faire une partie esgale a l'autre.

[. . . And finally, as for all other properties one may attribute to curved lines, these depend only on the magnitude of the angles they make with certain other lines. But when one can draw the straight lines which cut them at right angles, at the points where they (the curves) meet those (the lines) with which they make the angles one wishes to measure, or, which here I take to be the same, which cut their tangent lines; the magnitude of these angles is no harder to find than if they were contained between two straight lines. That is why I believe I will have set forth here everything that is required for the understanding of curved lines, when I have given the general method for drawing straight lines at right angles to any of their points which one may wish to choose. And I dare say that this is the most useful and most general problem not only that I know, but indeed that I have ever wished to know in geometry.

Let CE be the curved line, and let C be a point from which a line at right angles to it is to be drawn. I suppose that the thing has already been done, and that the desired line is CP, which I extend to the point P, where it meets the straight line GA, which I suppose to be that to whose points all points of the line CE are related. So that, letting MA or CB = y, and CM, or BA = x, I have some equation which explains the relation between x and y. Then I let PC = s and PA = v, or PM = $v - y$, and in reason of the right triangle PMC I have s^2, which is the square of the base equal to $x^2 + v^2 - 2vy + y^2$, which are the squares of the two sides. That is, I have $x = s^2 - v^2 + 2vy - y^2$, or else $y = v + s^2 - x^2$, and using this equation, I remove from the other equation which explained the relation of all points of the curve CE to those of the straight line GA, one of the two indeterminate quantities x or y. Which is easy to do by putting throughout $\sqrt{s^2 - v^2 + 2vy - y^2}$ instead of x, and the square of that sum instead of x^2, and its cube instead of x^3, and so on for the others, if it is x that I wish to remove; or else if it is y, by putting in its place $v + \sqrt{s^2 - x^2}$, and the square, or the cube, etc., of this sum, instead of y^2 or y^3 etc. So that after that there will always be one equation in which there remains only a single unknown quantity, x or y.

As if CE were an ellipse, and MA were the segment of its diameter, to which CM is applied as the ordinate, and which has r as its latus rectum, and q as the transverse axis, then by the thirteenth theorem of the first book of Apollonius, $x^2 = ry - \frac{r}{q}y^2$, from which removing x^2 there remains $s^2 - v^2 + 2vy - y^2 = ry - \frac{r}{q}y^2$. Or,

$$y^2 \frac{qry - 2qvy + qv^2 - qs^2}{q - r} \text{ equal to zero.}$$

For it is better here to consider in this way the whole sum than to make one part equal to the other].[3]

Less well known than Descartes, Guillaume de L'Hospital was a student of the Bernoullis and hence a friend of calculus as understood by Leibniz. His *Analyse des infiniment petits* of 1696 is apparently the first published textbook of differential calculus. In a remarkable preface the author presents a short history of the new analysis. He tries to do justice to Descartes, first, writing, "On sçait jusqu'où il a porté l'Analyse et la Géometrie, et combien l'alliage qu'il en a fait rend facile la solution d'une infinité de Problêmes qui paroissoient impénétrables avant luy" ["Everyone knows how far he advanced analysis and geometry and how much the mixture he made of them makes it easy to solve an infinite number of problems which seemed impenetrable before him"]. As for the new analysis, L'Hospital writes, "L'étenduë de ce calcul est immense: il convient aux Courbes mécaniques, comme aux géométriques; les signes radicaux luy sont indifferens, et même souvent commodes; il s'étend à tant d'indeterminées qu'on voudra.... Et de là naissent une infinité de découvertes surprenantes par rapport aux Tangentes tant courbes que droites..." ["The range of this calculus is immense: it can be used for mechanical as well as geometric curves; radical signs are indifferent to it, and indeed often helpful; it can be extended to as many unknowns as one may wish.... And from it are born an infinite number of surprising discoveries concerning curved and straight (?) tangent lines..."].[4]

L'Hospital's second section is entitled "Usage du calcul des différences pour trouver les Tangentes de toutes sortes de lignes courbes" ["Using differential calculus to find tangents to all sorts of curved lines"]. A final section is entitled "Nouvelle manière de se servir cu calcul des différences dans les courbes geometriques, d'où l'on déduit la Méthode de Mrs Descartes et Hudde" ["New method for using differential calculus in geometric curves, from which may be deduced the method of Messrs Descartes and Hudde"]. In the concluding paragraph of this final section, L'Hospital writes that he has shown how Descartes's and Hudde's method ought to be used (for such problems, precisely, as finding tangents and normals to conic-section and other curves), but that "l'on voit aussi en même temps qu'elle n'est pas comparable à celle de M. Leibnis, que j'ay tâché d'expliquer à fond dans ce Traitté: puisque cette derniére donne des résolutions générales où l'autre n'en fournit que de particulieres, qu'elle s'étend aux lignes Transcendantes, et qu'il n'est point nécessaire d'ôter les incommensurables; ce qui seroit tres souvent impraticable" ["at the same time it may be seen that it is not comparable to that of M. Leibniz, which I have tried to explain in depth in this treatise: since the latter method gives general solutions whereas the other only gives special ones, since it may be extended to transcendental lines, and since it is not necessary to remove the incommensurables, which last is often impossible in practice"].[5]

In his second section (on tangents), L'Hospital addresses himself to a problem precisely equivalent to the passage already quoted from

Descartes—that of finding the tangent (necessarily at right angles to the normal determined in Descartes's problem) to a given curve from a given point on the curve. L'Hospital writes:

PROPOSITION I.

Problême.

9. Soit une ligne courbe AM *telle que la relation de la coupée* AP *à l'appliquée* PM, *soit exprimée par une équation quelconque, et qu'il faille du point donné* M *sur cette courbe mener la tangente* MT.

Ayant mené l'appliquée *MP*, et supposé que la droite *MT* qui rencontre le diamètre au point *T*, soit la tangente cherchée; on concevra une autre appliquée *mp* infiniment proche de la première, avec une petite droite *MR* parallele à *AP*. Et en nommant les données *AP*, x; *PM*, y; (donc *Pp* ou *MR* = dx, et *Rm* = dy.) les triangles semblables *mRM* et *MPT* donneront *mR (dy)*. RM *(dx : : MP (y)* [sic]. PT = $\frac{ydx}{dy}$. Or par le moyen de la différence de l'équation donnee, on trouvera une valeur de *dx* en termes qui seront tous affectés par *dy*, laquelle étant multipliée par *y* & divisée par *dy*, donnera une valeur de la soutangente *PT* en termes entiére- ment connus et délivrés des différences, laquelle servira à mener la tangente cherchée *MT*. . . .

Exemple I.

11. 1°. Si l'on veut que *ay* [sic] = *yy* exprime la relation de *AP* à *PM;* la courbe *AM* fera une parabole qui aura pour paramétre la droite donnée *a,* et l'on aura en prenant de part et d'autre les dif- férences,

$$adx = 2ydy, \text{ et } dx = \frac{2ydy}{a}, \text{ et } PT \left(\frac{ydx}{dy}\right) = \frac{2yy}{a} = 2x \text{ en mettant}$$

pour *yy* sa valeur *ax*. D'où il faut que si l'on prend *PT* double de *AP*, et qu'on mene la droite *MT*, elle sera tangente au point *M*. Ce qui étoit proposé.

PROPOSITION I.

Problem.

9. Let AM *be a curved line such that the relation of the abscissa* AP *to the ordinate* PM *is expressed by a given equation; draw the tangent* MT *from the given point* M *on the curve.*

Having drawn the ordinate *MP*, and supposing that the straight line *MT* which meets the diameter in the point *T* is the desired tangent; we imagine another ordinate *mp* infinitely close to the first, with a small line *MR* parallel to *AP*. And naming the givens

AP, x; PM, y; (thus *Pp* or *MR* = *dx,* and *Rm* = *dy*) the similar triangles *mRM* and *MPT* will give *mR (dy)*. *RM (dy* : : *MP (y)* [*sic*]. *PT* =$\frac{ydx}{dy}$, Differentiating the given equation, we find a value of *dx* in terms which are all affected by *dy,* which value being multiplied by *y* and divided by *dy,* will give a value of the subtangent *PT* in terms entirely known and free from derivatives, which will serve to draw the desired tangent *MT.* . . .

Example I.

11. 1°. If we say that *ay* [*ax?*] = *y²* expresses the relation of *AP* to *PM;* the curve *AM* will make a parabola which will have as its parameter the given line *a,* and, differentiating on both sides we have the derivatives, *adx* = *2ydy,* and *dx* = *2ydy* and *PT* $(\frac{ydx}{dy})$ = $\frac{2y^2}{a}$ = *2x,* substituting for *y²* its value *ax.* From which it follows that if one takes *PT* double to *AP* and one draws the line *MT,* it will be tangent to the point *M.* Which was the desired result].[6]

Leaving aside the obvious differences in language, spelling, and printing conventions between the two texts, the reader will quickly note considerable differences in what Descartes and L'Hospital believe they may take for granted in their audience. For his part, Descartes uses not the Viètian notation but a system generally attributed to himself. Just as Descartes's fencing master tended to name the adversaries in his *Académie de l'espee* Abraham and Zacharie, Descartes habitually uses *x, y,* and *z* for unknown quantities and earlier letters of the alphabet— often *a, b,* and *c,* but here *s* and *v*—for known quantities. This notation leads naturally to the notion of *x* and *y* axes intersecting in an origin point, as these are generally understood in analytic geometry today— although Descartes himself merely makes them equal to certain lines on his figure, implying "quelque equation, qui explique le rapport qui est entre *x* et *y.*" Already in Descartes, however, the function of the *x* and *y* axes remains constant, even though in the present problem the equation must be solved for *s* or *v,* rather than for *x* or *y* to obtain the desired quantity for construction of a normal to the curve. In L'Hospital's problem, the Cartesian notation, the equation defining the curve in terms of *x* and *y,* abscissa and ordinate, are taken for granted, simply appearing in the givens of the problem as "une ligne courbe . . . exprimée par une équation quelconque. . . ." Often, although not in this particular case, L'Hospital's figures show axes and an origin point independent of the curve and the tangent, normal, or other constructed lines related to it. In the same way Descartes takes considerable space to explain the operation of substitution of x and y in his equation, "en mettant partout $\sqrt{ss - vv + 2vy - yy}$ au lieu d'x, et le quarré de cete somme au lieu d'xx, et son cube au lieu d'x^3, et ainsi des autres)" and repeats the same instructions in almost as much detail for y. L'Hospital, on the other hand, although writing a textbook for a presumably less sophisticated audience, assumes much greater familiarity with simple algebraic operations, skipping several steps in his exposition and explaining only his substitution of ax for y^2. This last explanation, moreover, is more a reminder of one possibility of substitution than an explanation of the operation of substitution itself, thereby further demonstrating L'Hospital's and his audience's additional sixty years of experience with algebra and analytic geometry.

Clearly, L'Hospital's exposition also profits from a variety of other innovations in mathematics in the period between 1637 and 1696. In addition to Descartes, L'Hospital mentions several other seventeenth-century mathematicians in his preface. And his method quoted above, based on the notion of similar triangles rather than the Pythagorean theorem as used by Descartes, is closer to Fermat's solution of the same problem than to Descartes's. Among other advantages, the similar-triangles method permits L'Hospital, as he himself suggests in his preface, to eliminate radical signs from the results, allowing a simple and more "elegant" solution. In the last section of his book, L'Hospital returns to the problem of tangents to conic-section and other curves, and this time uses a method based on the work of Hudde to resolve the resulting equations, a method dependent on the necessity of these equations having equal multiple roots at the point of intersection of the tangent and the curve.[7] L'Hospital's principal methodological advance is, of course, his use of differential calculus. In the example quoted above, L'Hospital's dx and dy encapsulate a whole complex of assumptions and operations (explained to his reader in the first section), which have proved to be the wave of the future in mathematical analysis.

It is these last two types of differences, certainly which have led such writers as Yvon Belaval, in his brilliant *Leibniz critique de Descartes*—or Michel Serres, in his *Hermes,* his *Leibniz,* and elsewhere—to minimize Descartes's contribution to modern mathematics in favor of Leibniz and, by implication, such successors as the Bernoullis and L'Hospital. Descartes's book is not entitled *Géométrie analytique,* but simply *Géométrie.*

Throughout the book Descartes's point of reference is what he calls the "Geometrie commune" or the "Geometrie ordinaire" as practiced by "les anciens." Descartes presents his work as more generally applicable and labor-saving (all mathematicians present their work as general and labor-saving with respect to their predecessors) with respect to those same ancient geometers: with its help, ". . . on peut construire tous les Problemes de la Geometrie ordinaire, sans faire autre chose que le peu qui est compris dans les quatre figures que j'ay expliquées. Ce que je ne croy pas que les anciens ayent remarqué. Car autrement ils n'eussent pas pris la peine d'en escrire tant de gros livres, ou le seul ordre de leurs propositions nous fait connoistre qu'ils n'ont point eu la vraye methode pour les trouver toutes, mais qu'ils ont seulement ramassé celles qu'ils ont rencontrées" ["one may construct all the problems of ordinary geometry, without doing anything but the little that is included in the four figures I have explicated. Which is something I do not believe the ancients noticed, for otherwise they would not have taken the trouble to write so many heavy books, in which even the order of their propositions shows us that they did not have the true method for finding all of them, but only picked up those they happened to encounter"].[8]

In this context Belaval is no doubt correct in suggesting that Descartes is the inventor not of "analytic geometry" but merely of "algebraic geometry." Indeed Belaval goes to some length to show that even if Descartes may have used such notions as limit or functionality or even infinitesimals or integration to resolve specific problems, the general implications of these concepts escaped him. In a passage praised by Serres, Belaval summarizes, more or less as quoted above, Descartes's solution of the problem of the normal to a curve and compares it unfavorably with Fermat's "méthode déjà différentielle" ["already differential method"]. Elsewhere, Belaval declares confidently, referring to Descartes's treatment of the tangent to a logarithmic curve, that "personne ne contestera que Descartes n'invente là une technique pour résoudre un problème d'équation différentielle. Mais ce qui est conforme à son génie inventif, se révèle aussitôt contraire à son génie philosophique: sa philosophie fait obstacle à la considération de l'infinitésimal" ["no one will dispute that Descartes here invents a technique for resolving a differential equation problem. But what serves his inventive genius immediately reveals itself contrary to his philosophical genius: his philosophy resists consideration of the infinitesimal"].[9]

When considered in light of an accumulative model of mathematical discovery, such a comparison clearly bestows the certificate of merit on Fermat and, by implication, on Fermat's successors in differentiation, Newton and Leibniz—since it was for Leibniz that all the various presumably essential elements of the calculus fell together into a coherent method, later disseminated by L'Hospital. When considered in terms of alternative historical models, however, even the detailed demonstration of Belaval takes on a very different meaning, which goes beyond the accumulation of mathematical advances to something like the crisis-and-response model of Kuhn or the successive-stages model applied to literary texts in preceding chapters.

The most striking evidence in favor of such a view is the context in which both Descartes and L'Hospital presented their work—in the similarities, rather than the differences, between the two solutions. Actually, although the problem of the normal (or tangent) to a given point on a curve was resolved by purely geometric means in antiquity (by Apollonius of Pergusa), it enjoyed a striking renewal of interest in the seventeenth century, as part of a very general renewal of interest in conic sections and an increase of interest (which one might, if one wished, somehow describe as baroque) in curved lines in general. The most casual paging through of the geometries of such earlier writers as Viète, or Stevin, or Peletier du Mans reveals problems (and figures) treating straight lines and circles in large numbers, with few or no examples of conic-section or more complicated curves. Descartes himself suggests in a passage of the *Géométrie* that "Il est vray qu'ils [les Anciens] n'ont pas aussy entierement receu les sections coniques en leur Geometrie" ["It is also true that they (the Ancients) never fully received conic sections into their geometry"]. In contrast, in the years between Viète and Leibniz, solutions to the problem of the normal (or tangent) to a curve were offered not only by Descartes and Fermat, but also by a considerable number of others. Fermat's friend and correspondent Beaugrand, for example, gave a method somewhat different from Fermat's but in his view "plus simple, facile, et generale" ["simpler, easier, and more general"] than Descartes's. Two other methods are offered by Huygens, who in turn comments on solutions by Sluse and Hudde. Other methods or variations were presented in the same period by Roberval, in his *Traité des indivisibles* and elsewhere, and by Torricelli, Barrow, and perhaps Wallis, in addition to those eventually proposed by Newton and Leibniz and presented in the *Analyse des infiniment petits* by L'Hospital. This list, based on my merely casual inventory of the possibilities, is probably not exhaustive. It is sufficient, however, to suggest that a type of problem that seemed to hold no unusual interest for sixteenth-century geometers came to occupy the attention of a great many mathematicians in the following century.[10]

In such numerous company, the limitations of Descartes's understanding of functionality are less significant than his clear awareness, shared with other mathematicians of the period, that "il est mieux en cet endroit de considerer ensemble toute la somme, que d'en faire une partie esgale a l'autre." In the same way L'Hospital's semi-Cartesian or Hudde-ian concern with multiple identical roots, presented as a method of deducing Cartesian solutions from Leibniz, is actually discussed by Descartes himself in the *Géométrie* when he suggests that "lorsqu'il y a deux racines esgales en une equation" ["when there are two equal roots in an equation"] various operations can make the two members of the equation correspond term by term.[11]

Descartes's hesitant treatment of infinitesimals, moreover, is simply one discussion among a great many contemporary ones that address and give one or another solution to the same sort of problem. During Boyer's "Century of Anticipation" such mathematicians as Stevin, Kepler, Galileo, Cavalieri, Torricelli, and Roberval, among others, all used various elements of what was to become infinitesimal calculus or resolved problems using a theoretical rationale similar—but presumably inferior—to what would later be used by Newton and Leibniz. Newton's "ultimate ratios" and "fluxions" and Leibniz's "vanishing quantities," presented in the text above as L'Hospital's "autre apliquée *mp* infiniment proche de la premiere" ["other ordinate *mp* infinitely close to the first"] were preceded over a considerable period by the similar notion of "indivisibles." Indivisibles appeared in so many slightly varying forms among seventeenth-century mathematicians that Pascal—who himself presents varying views on the subject—refers ironically to those quantities with which "indivisibilium studiosis familiaria sunt" ["those who study indivisibles are familiar"] and to all those who "in indivisibilium doctrinâ tantisper versati sunt" ["are even slightly well versed in the doctrine of indivisibles"].[12] Indeed, close reading of Newton and Leibniz, those inventors or discoverers for whom all the indispensable elements fell together, shows that these giants also varied or made vague statements concerning the theoretical justification of their methods. Sometimes indeed they seem to hark back to the theoretically disappointing indivisibles of their predecessors, or even to purely geometrical proofs, presumably more familiar and reassuring to seventeenth-century readers, in presenting their conclusions.

Taken on balance, the limited generality of Descartes's methods is perhaps less suggestive of the mathematical context in which he worked than his optimistic statement, elsewhere in the *Géométrie*, that "Mesme encore que les poins de la ligne courbe ne se rapportassent pas en la façon que jay ditte a ceux d'une ligne droite, mais en toute autre qu'on sçauroit imaginer, on ne laisse pas de pouvoir tousjours avoir une telle equation" ["Even if the points of the curve do not relate to a straight line in the way I have said, but in any other way one might wish to imagine, there is still always some way to find such an equation"].[13] And Descartes's limited realization of the benefits of calculus is surely less suggestive, in the mathematical context of his times, than his eloquent affirmation that "pour ce qui est de toutes les autres proprietés qu'on peut attribuer aux lignes courbes, elles ne dependent que de la grandeur des angles qu'elles font avec quelques autres lignes. . . . Et j'ose dire que c'est cecy le probleme le plus utile, et le plus general non seulement que je sçache, mais mesme que j'ay jamais desiré de sçavoir. . . . " Descartes's statement is echoed, moreover, by another later and much more advanced worker in the same mathematical paradigm, L'Hospital, when he writes in his preface that first among the advantages of the new analysis is its application to "une infinité de découvertes surprenantes par rapport aux Tangentes tant courbes que droites. . . . "

Agreeing with Belaval's conclusion that Descartes's mathematical innovation was extremely limited compared with Leibniz's, Serres writes that any Cartesian revolution in mathematics "n'a pas lieu pour le *contenu* de ce modèle: la mathématique cartésienne reste hellénique, c'est-à-dire métrique et réductible, en un sens, à une théorie des proportions. . . . le révolutionnaire cache un sévère conservateur" ["does not affect the contents of this model: Cartesian mathematics remains hellenic, that is, metric and reducible, in a sense, to a theory of proportions. . . . the revolutionary hides a severe conservative"]. Serres adds, however, that Descartes is nevertheless the agent of a revolution in the "situation" of mathematics. He writes: "Révolutionnaire, Descartes l'est pour ce qui concerne la *situation* des Mathématiques: Leur fécondité est indépendante de la Logique stérile de l'Ecole. Le modèle est autonome par rapport à une discipline qu'on rejette, de même que l'ordre philosophique se libère d'une théodicée d'où a disparu le monde intelligible, ou que la démarche du sujet connaissant est déliée d'un système du savoir, formel et pré-établi" ["Descartes is indeed revolutionary as regards the *situation* of mathematics. The model is autonomous with respect to a discipline that is being rejected, just as the philosophical order liberates itself from a theodicy from which the intelligible world has disappeared, or the quest of the perceiving object is freed from a system of knowledge that is formal and preestablished"].[14]

It is worth noting, however, that if Descartes was a revolutionary, he was certainly not a lonely one. Instead, he is one of several to adopt a superior, post-Viètian notation system. He is also one of several to approach, in one way or another, the notions of functionality, of curved-line analysis, and, of course, the elusive infinitesimals. In priority-of-invention terms Descartes is no doubt simply someone who failed to invent the calculus; in Kuhnian terms, however, he appears somewhat differently. For although Kuhn himself is in the habit of consecrating great men by naming scientific revolutions after them, there are nevertheless certain stages in the Kuhnian model in which a great many workers are doing approximately the same thing at the same time. These are the crisis stages, when many workers are casting about for a new paradigm, and the assimilation stages, in which many people are working out the consequences of a paradigm change. Descartes would seem to fit admirably into one of these stages, along with Fermat, Hudde, Sluse, and the rest. And if all these workers appear as casters-about with respect to invention of the calculus, they also appear as participants in an assimilation stage, as practitioners of Kuhnian "normal science" with respect to post-Viètian notation, functionality, curved-line analysis, and any Serres-ian revolution in the "situation" of mathematics.

In Foucaldian terms, meanwhile, Descartes appears as one of those fortunate enough to exploit a newly created mathematical space, one in which his proofs differ less from those of Fermat, or Huyghens, or Beaugrand than they do from Viète and Peletier du Mans. As Descartes himself grudgingly acknowledged, Fermat's solution to the problem of the tangent to a curve may have been more advanced than his own, as may Beaugrand's or some other's. All of these writers, however, pose the same problems and struggle with the same issues. And even L'Hospital's solution, so much more advanced than the others, is not different, but rather subsumes them, makes them deducible from itself. Under these conditions a Kuhnian might well see the invention of calculus itself as simply one stage of the "normal science" working out of some Cartesian revolution. And a Foucaldian might argue that the invention of calculus was likewise merely one inevitable result of the exploitation of a new *épistémè*.

Actually, this chapter is the first to concern itself at all with the matter of *who* the revolutionary in a given field may have been—a false problem in literary studies and perhaps a false problem in the history of science, even in Kuhnian "revolutionary" science history. The preceding chapters have suggested, instead, that "Cartesian" problems were dealt with by Thibault, that "Cornelian" problems were dealt with by Honoré d'Urfé and Schélandre, that "Larochefoucaldian" problems were foreshadowed by Charron and others. In some working-out stage of seventeenth-century intellect, just as Descartes is a contemporary of Corneille, so Newton and Leibniz are precise contemporaries of Racine, Boileau, La Fontaine, Molière, and the other greats of the so-called "classical moment." And in such a schema, L'Hospital is something like the post-Racinian tragedians, something like a La Grange-Chancel or Longepierre of mathematics, exploiting "normal literature" or "normal mathematics" after the dust of any presumed revolution has cleared away.

Analysis of this kind, in some working-out period of the middle and later seventeenth century might well be extended to other scientific domains, as the studies of Alexandre Koyré or Helen E. Metzger, among others, abundantly suggest. My unsystematic reading among the scientific treatises of a university library suggests that assimilation of the "new science" of the Renaissance and seventeenth century may be observed to move very slowly indeed, not only in the poets but also in scientific textbooks themselves. An example might be Father Bourdin's *Cours de mathematique* of 1661. Bourdin still describes, in his astronomical section, the "supposition des anciens," the "supposition de Copernic," and the "supposition de Tycho." He adds naïvely—or disingenuously—that the latter is "celle qui est aujourd'hui en vogue." Sebastien Le Clerc's *Practique de la geometrie* of 1691 expresses the same hesitation between Ptolmaic, Copernican, and Brahian conceptions—just as, in the 1670s, spectators and critics sometimes hesitated between the *Phèdres* of Racine and Jacques Pradon.[15]

NOTES

1. Boyer, *History of the Calculus* (New York: Dover, 1949 and 1959), p. 98. See also Viète, *Opera Mathematica* (Hildesheim: G. Olms, 1970).

2. Boyer, *History of the Calculus*, p. 96.

3. Descartes, *Géométrie* (orig. publ. 1637; La Salle, Ill.: Open Court, 1952), pp. 93–97 (orig. ed., pp. 341–43). Translation is by the author.

4. L'Hospital, *Analyse des infiniment petits* (Paris: Imp. royale, 1696), sig. iii r°, iv v°.

5. Ibid., pp. 11, 164, 181.

6. Ibid., pp. 11–12, also 167–68, 172–76, 181.

7. Ibid.˙

8. Belaval, *Leibniz critique de Descartes* (Paris: Gallimard, 1960), p. 304, also pp. 300–313. Serres, *Hermes*, 1 (Paris: Seuil, 1968), pp. 140–49, 58, 67, 85, 99, 131; and his *Le Système de Leibniz et ses modèles mathématiques*, 1 (Paris: P.U.F., 1968), pp. 151–63. Descartes, *Géométrie*, p. 16.

9. Belaval, *Leibniz*, pp. 305, 310. See Serres, *Hermes*, 1: 146–47.

10. Descartes, *Géométrie*, p. 42 (orig. ed., p. 316). See Evelyn Walker, *A Study of the Traité des indivisibles of Gilles Persone de Roberval*... (New York: Teachers College, 1932), pp. 124–41.

11. Descartes, *Géométrie*, p. 105 (orig. ed., 347).

12. Boyer, *History of the Calculus*, pp. 96–186. Pascal, *Oeuvres complètes* (Paris: Seuil, 1963), p. 94.

13. Descartes, *Géométrie*, p. 98 (orig. ed., p. 344).

14. Serres, *Hermes*, I, 140.

15. Bourdin, *Cours de mathématiques* (Paris, 1661), pp. 126, 128, 130.

CHAPTER 9

Two Modes of Metaphorical Unity:
L'Innocence descouverte
and *Phèdre*

WHETHER IN SPITE of or because of aesthetic trends, literary subjects clearly have a life of their own. Don Juan or the mad scientist or the amorous priest or the detective enter literary history at a given epoch and undergo divers modifications before, perhaps, disappearing from the literary cosmos. In the sixteenth and seventeenth centuries the story of Sophonisbe and the story of Medea enjoyed a considerable vogue in successive versions by Mellin de Saint-Gelais, Montchrestien, Montreux, Mairet, Corneille, and Longepierre, among others. The same is true, of course, of the numerous sixteenth- and seventeenth-century plays based on the legend of Phaedra.

Certain major elements of this legend—Phaedra's more or less incestuous love for Theseus's son Hippolyte, her deliberations with her nurse or confidante, her declaration of love, Theseus's return and presumption of Hippolyte's guilt, Theseus's prayer for divine retribution, and the returning messenger's account of the innocent Hippolyte's tragic death, provoked by a monster risen from the sea—are well known. French dramatic versions of the story in the period range from Robert Garnier's *Hippolyte* of 1573, through a 1591 text by Jean Yeuwain, and later versions by Guérin de la Pinelière (*Hippolyte,* 1635), Gabriel Gilbert (*Hypolite ou le Garçon insensible,* 1647), and Mathieu Bidar (*Hippolyte,* 1675), until Racine's masterpiece of 1677 and its competing play of the same date by Pradon.[1]

Careful comparison of all these texts might constitute something like a summary of the evolution suggested by the preceding chapters. Thus Garnier's 1573 version presents something very like the Renaissance— or mannerist or even baroque—worldview of Ronsard's sonnet describing Saint-Cosme. Certainly Hippolyte's death, as recounted by Garnier's messenger, takes place in a world of richly developed metaphors and signs, with allusions to the North winds, mariners, shepherds, hunters, whirlwinds, plowmen, and even vintners:

> Comme quand en esté le ciel se courrouçant
> Noircist, esclaire, bruit, les hommes menaçant,
> Le pauvre vigneron présagist par tels signes,
> S'outrageant l'estomac, le malheur de ses vignes;
> Aussi tost vient la gresle ainsi que drageons blancs
> Batre le sainct Bacchus à la teste et aux flancs,
> Le martelle de coups, et boutonne la terre
> De ses petits raisins enviez du tonnerre.
> Ainsi faisoit ce monstre . . .

[Just as, when in summer the sky is angered and blackened, threatening men with thunder and lightning, the poor vintner predicts by such signs, an outrage to his entrails, the misfortune of his vines; soon comes the hail like white dragons to beat holy Bacchus on the head and flanks, hammering with blows and covering the earth with tiny grapes like buttons coveted by the thunder. Thus also did the monster . . .]. (Garnier, pp. 316–17).

Yeuwain's 1591 play continues in the same tradition of mannerist or baroque incarnation. It also shows a greater degree of epistemological concern. Garnier's play began with a prologue in which Aegeus, returning from hell, states that "Je sors de l'Achéron, d'où les ombres des morts/Ne ressortent jamais couvertes de leurs corps" ["I come from the Achéron, from which the shadows of the dead never return covered with their bodies"] (Garnier, p. 247). Yeuwain, however, begins with a relatively more epistemologically oriented monologue by Hippolyte: "Allés, enceignés moy ces forés ombrageuses./Questés par-cy par-là, sur les cimes rameuses . . . " ["Go, stake out for me these shadowy forests./Seek here and there on the leafy summits . . . "] (Yeuwain, p. 7).

Yeuwain's text also offers a well nigh overpowering element of baroque horror—another form of epistemological distancing, as previously suggested. Thus his messenger's speech is much longer than Garnier's. The mariners, shepherds, and vintner are replaced by references to certain mountain summits, "Qu'ont rendus si fameux maints sanglans homicides" ["Made so famous by many bloody homicides"] (Yeuwain, p. 73), and the like. Yeuwain describes the destruction of Hippolyte's body in unusual detail, restoring items from Seneca's Latin version omitted by Garnier and embroidering on Seneca's already bloody description in a twenty-seven-line text. As if this were not enough, the messenger's description returns for a remarkable reprise in act 5. As in Seneca's version, the remains of Hippolyte's body are brought onstage before Theseus. His anguished monologue, as adapted by Yeuwain, embellishes on Seneca's:

> O pere infortuné . . .
> . . . tasche au-moins d'arranger,
> De ce corps déchiré les pièces sanglantéës,
> Et les remettre au lieu, dont elles sont ostéës.
> Céte épaule robuste icy mettre se doit.
> Icy du dextre flanc ie remarq[ue] l'endroit;
> Et céte gauche habile, icy doit estre mise,
> A serrer, et lascher la resne bien aprise.

[O unfortunate father, try at least to arrange the bloody pieces of this torn body and put them back whence they were taken. This robust shoulder should go here. Here I see the place for the right side, and the left hand, well taught to hold and to let go the rein, should go here]. (Yeuwain, p. 88).

Thus commenting on the relation of parts to wholes as well as on the body animate and inanimate, Theseus reflects on the enormity of his task of reconstruction and finally sends his servants back to look for missing pieces of the unfortunate Hippolyte.

Guérin de la Pinelière's *Hippolyte* of 1635 resembles Schélandre's *Tyr et Sidon* of 1628 in the sense that it combines metaphorical and classificatory epistemological preoccupations. Described by critic Claude Francis as the "baroque" *Phèdre*, the play's consensus baroque elements are framed and controlled in the manner of *L'Illusion comique* or *Le Menteur* or *Le Véritable Saint Genest* or, again, Schélandre's later version of *Tyr et Sidon*. After a prologue, La Pinelière's text begins with a speech in which Phaedra describes the confused nature of her thought processes. The horror of the messenger's recital includes an eye impaled upon a thorn but is shorter and less emphatic than Yeuwain's. Elsewhere, when Theseus declares that men are too easily influenced by their surroundings, he applies this view to a hierarchy of gods and princes. Phaedra herself describes royalty as the "Lieutenans de ces grands Roys des Cieux" ["Lieutenants of these great kings of the skies"] (La Pinelière, p. 25).

In Gabriel Gilbert's *Hypolite* of 1647 the balance shifts strikingly in the direction of law, reason, classification, prudence, and Cartesianism.

Gilbert's Phaedra makes much of the fact that she and Theseus are not yet legally married, so that her passion for Hippolyte is technically not incest or even adultery. Moreover, she correctly perceives that Theseus is in love with a certain Céphise, whose city he seeks to conquer. Phaedra concludes lucidly that "Je puis abandonner celuy qui m'abandonne,/La raison le permet, et l'equité l'ordonne" ["I can abandon someone who abandons me,/Reason allows it and equity requires it"] (Gilbert, p. 5). Hippolyte himself, in clear contrast to his chaste and mysogynist predecessors, is capable of love and is in fact in love with Phaedra, whose advances he discourages only out of respect for his father. When Theseus accuses him, Hippolyte defends himself in a confrontation scene significantly absent from earlier versions of the legend. His self-justification is based squarely on notions of classification, progression, and verisimilitude:

> Le crime qu'on m'impute est grand, est effroyable,
> Mais si mal inventé qu'il n'est pas vrai-semblable,
>
> . . . . .
>
> L'on me nomme ennemi de l'amour et des femmes;
> Et l'on me nomme amant, l'on accuse mes flames,
> Peut-on me reprocher l'insensibilité,
> M'accuser de froideur, et d'impudicité;
> Si j'aprouve à grand'peine une ardeur legitime,
> La pourrai-je aprouver quand elle est jointe au crime:
> Mon coeur n'est point bruslé de feux incestueux,
> Si j'avois de l'amour, il seroit vertueux.
> Cette accusation est pleine d'injustice,
> Comparez seulement mes moeurs avec ce vice:
> Vous verrez que c'est moy qui suis seul offencé.
> Pour juger du present, r'appelez le passé...

[The crime of which I am accused is grave, is frightful, but so badly invented that it lacks verisimilitude....I'm said to be an enemy of love and women, and I'm said to be a lover, I am accused of love; can they reproach me with insensitivity, accuse me of coldness along with impudicity; if I can hardly approve of a legitimate ardor, could I approve one that was linked to crime: my heart does not burn with incestuous fires; if I were in love, my love would be virtuous. This accusation is full of injustice—simply compare my morals with this vice. You will see that it is I alone who am offended. To judge the present, just recall the past ..."]. (Gilbert, pp. 89–90).

Similar elements appear in Mathieu Bidar's *Hippolyte* of 1675, in which Hippolyte loves the princess Cyane, despite an unmarried Phaedra's highly lucid attempts to separate them and the lovers' rational attempts to defend themselves. Bidar's Hippolyte dies as he does his intelligent best to resolve a difficult situation. His story is tragic only in the modern and relatively trivial sense of a miscarriage of justice—a sense solidly grounded in the *épistémè* of classification and astute calculation of self-interest.

Taken as a group, all these plays represent movement from a world of harmony, resemblance, and fatality to a world of reason, legalism, representation, and contingency. Curiously, in narrative semiotic terms the actantial distribution, after a certain date, consistently gives Hippolyte an object of affection and an adjuvant to help him and defend him in his endeavors. Beginning with Gilbert's 1647 version of the legend, these plays consistently replace the narrative semiotic function of destination—Diane's influence on Hippolyte and Venus's influence on Phaedra—with mediation, in which reason, courtiership, contingency, and other possibilities of the repertoire of practical or prudent reason may succeed or fail to carry the day.

THESE several versions of the Phaedra legend thus represent consistent changes in language, dramaturgy, period-style categories, actantial distribution, narrative function, and epistemological assumptions in the period between 1573 and 1675. At the same time further analysis would show changes in those underlying concerns that give structure and unity to each of the several texts. Such underlying concerns might be studied according to any one of a number of methods: they might be analyzed in structuralist terms of one kind or another; they might be analyzed in terms of "deep structure" as presented by A. J. Greimas and others. In the present instance, however, the analysis with the most time-specific implications for notions of intellectual movement may be study of the metaphorical unity or inner coherence presented by J. D. Hubert, in his *Essai d'exégèse racinienne,* as the "seule règle technique à laquelle les auteurs ne dérogent jamais" ["sole technical rule which the authors never infringe"] in the seventeenth century.[2] To the extent that a particular form of underlying structure—in this case, Hubert's metaphorical unity—may be specific to a given epoch of French literature and discourse, it could be expected to evolve through or at the beginning and end of that period. A study of the metaphorical unity of the plays described above might be very long indeed; some idea of the situation may be derived, however, from study of two other versions of the Phaedra legend, rather widely separated in time, Jean Auvray's *Marfilie* or *L'Innocence descouverte* of 1609 (reprinted, apparently, in 1628) and Jean Racine's masterpiece *Phèdre* of 1677.[3]

Auvray's play is not mentioned in Antoine Adam's *Histoire de la littérature française au dix-septième siècle.* Carrington Lancaster's reference in his voluminous *History of French Dramatic Literature in the Seventeenth Century* is terse. *L'Innocence descouverte* is, he says, one of four extant tragicomedies from the reign of Henri IV that may "represent the kind of tragi-comedy that was to be written by Alexandre Hardy. . . ."[4] In any case, Auvray's tragicomedy is of the kind that, in addition to resolving a tragic situation happily, also mixes serious and comic scenes — the sort of tragicomedy that was admired by the possibly baroque apologist François Ogier.

Written in a dramatic style situated somewhere between the minimally plotted and lyrical monologue plays of the late sixteenth century and the more strongly plotted and dialogued seventeenth-century style, *L'Innocence descouverte* presents a Roman nobleman's aging wife Marfilie, who falls in love with a stepson, Fabrice. Marfilie languishes and consults a kind of semilyrical, semifarcical doctor, accompanied by her nurse and an idiot servant, Thomas. Marfilie declares her love to Fabrice, who, hoping to improve his stepmother's health, pretends to respond to her advances. When Marfilie discovers the deception, she flies into a rage and decides to poison Fabrice. Thomas is sent back to the doctor with a large sum of money to buy poison, an errand he interrupts to consult the doctor about a gigantic, musical, and presumably comical *pet* he passed the night before. Marfilie's plans are foiled, meanwhile, when the doctor gives Thomas a sleeping potion instead of poison. She is doubly or triply foiled, moreover, when her own son Anthoine drinks the medicine instead of Fabrice. Anthoine falls into a coma, and Marfilie decides to accuse Fabrice of poisoning him. Fabrice's innocence is discovered, however, when the doctor comes to testify at the trial. The executioner releases Fabrice, and Marfilie and her servants are condemned to exile.

Despite its simple plot and apparently superficial comic passages, *L'Innocence descouverte* expresses opinions on a variety of philosophical subjects. Judging by their affirmations, Auvray's personages of 1609 (or 1628) are solidly rooted in a worldview based on sympathy and antipathy, a certain awareness of scientific advances notwithstanding. Thus Fabrice explains that before he could truly accept Marfilie's love,

> Plustost en la nature on trouvera du vuide
> La terre deviendra transparente et lucide,
> Plustost l'ours vollera par la vague des airs,
> L'Aigle approche-soleil plustost fendra les mers,
> Le coq, et le lyon n'auront d'antipathie:
> La vigne avec l'ormeau n'aura de sympathie,
> Bref, tout retombera en l'antique chaos.

[Rather we will find a vacuum in nature, the earth will become transparent and brilliant, rather the bear will fly on the waves of the air, the sun-approaching eagle will rather cleave the seas, the cock and the lion will cease their antipathy: the vine with the elm will no longer have sympathy—in brief, all will fall back into the ancient chaos].[5]

In the play's last act a magistrate invokes the sun in a manner clearly implying baroque incarnation as well as geocentric cosmology, as he apostrophizes the "beau Soleil, claire lampe du monde" ["great Sun, bright lamp of the world"], which daily makes a "tour continuel de la machine ronde" ["continual circle around the round machine"]. In the same passage the magistrate praises his calling in terms that suggest he sees it, too, primarily in metaphorical terms. He asks the sun rhetorically if, as it moves around the world, it sees anything more precious than "la sainte Justice." Sacred Justice, he continues, is "Le ciment glutineux des estats monarchiques" ["The glutinous cement of monarchical states"]. Without justice, moreover,

> Tout iroit derechef en l'antique desordre
> L'aspre avec l'applani, le bas avec le hault
> L'Humide avec le sec, le froid avec le chaud
> La nuict avec le jour, le ciel avec la terre
> Se livreroit sans cesse une intestine guerre.

[All would return immediately to the ancient disorder, the rough with the smooth, the low with the high, the wet with the dry, the cold with the hot, night with day, earth with sky would give themselves up to internecine war.] (pp. 45–46).

For Fabrice, God is that highly personified being who "au bout de son doit soustient la terre en bransle" ["on his fingertip supports the moving world"] (p. 25). At the same time, however, *L'Innocence descouverte* offers very few suggestions of an alternative view. Thus in act 5, the First Counselor also suggests that there is no more divine quality than justice but expresses his praise in different terms than his previously quoted colleague. For the First Counselor, justice is the very essence of the grandeur of God. He quotes Cicero to the effect that justice is a mirror in which man can contemplate the image of the gods themselves: "Car Dieu ne seroit Dieu, sans ceste qualité,/La deité deffaut où deffaut l'equité" ["God would not be God, without that quality; divinity is missing where equity is lacking"] (pp. 40–41). Similarly, although Marfilie's doctor believes that the origin of illness is sin, he is also scientific enough to see God as an essentially orderly creator. God's justice is such, he says, that He has "Donné à chasque mal son propre alexitaire" ["given to each malady its palliative"] (p. 14).

Auvray's essentially metaphorical worldview is also expressed in the structure and unity of the play itself, that is, its specifically metaphorical unity. Like those plays studied in light of their "inner coherence" by Hubert, *L'Innocence descouverte* carries in its initial lines metaphorical notions that reappear in various forms throughout the text. Mixing ordinary plot exposition with metaphorical exposition, *L'Innocence descouverte* begins with a monologue by Marfilie:

> Quel feu rampe en mon coeur? quelle flame cruelle,
> Furetans dans mes os, consume leur moüelle?
> Seroit-ce toy, Amour, implacable bourreau,
> Sorcier seroit-ce toy qui d'un philtre nouveau
> Ensorcelle mes sens? non non ta chaude flame,
> Ne pourroit eschauffer les glaces de mon ame:
> Mon Avril est passé, je courbe sous le poix
> De mes ans escoulez à grand peine ma voix
> Exprime les conceps de mon esprit languide,
> Ià mon front crystallin de mainte noire ride
> N'est plus comme il souloit le louvre et le sejour,
> Des graces, des beautez de Cypris et d'Amour:
> Mes joües ne sont plus neigeusement pourprines,
> Et le Corail besson de mes levres sucrines,
> Palle ne semond plus un amoureux baiser
> Qui pouvoit les plus froids doucement embraser,
> Bref je ne semble plus qu'une tronche animee,
> Qu'un phantosme ombrageux, qu'une idole enfumee,
> Dont le moite cerveau distille incessamment

Par ses canaux communs un foetide excrement:
Et toutesfois ie sens vne flame traistresse
Brusler honteusement ceste morne vieillesse:
Ah! vrayement c'est Amour, ie recognoy ses traits,
Sa blessure, son feu, son amorce, et ses rets,
Reths, amorces, feu, traits donc cruel il fait guerre
Au ciel et à l'Enfer, à l'air et à la terre.

[What fire crawls in my heart? what cruel flame, ferreting in my bones, consumes their marrow? Is it you, love, merciless executioner, is it you, sorcerer, who with a new philter enchant my senses? No, no, your hot flame cannot heat up the ices of my soul: My April is past, I am bent beneath the weight of my transpired years, with great difficulty my voice expresses the concepts of my languid spirit; already my forehead, faceted by so many black wrinkles, is no longer, as it was, the palace and the resting place of the graces, of the beauties of Cypris and of love; my cheeks are no longer snowy purple, and the twin coral of my sugared lips, pale, no longer summons up an amorous kiss, which could turn the coldest to fire; in short, I seem no longer more than a living log, a shadowy phantom, a smoky idol, whose humid brain incessantly distills, by its common tubes, a fetid excrement; and yet I sense a traitorous flame, burning shamefully in this, my melancholy old age! Ah, indeed, it is Love, I recognize his arrows, his wound, his fire, his bait, and his net; net, baits, fire, arrows, thus cruelly he makes war on the sky and on hell, on air and earth] (pp. 1–2).

Read as exposition, the preceding passage introduces the play's major personage, Marfilie, and at the same time introduces two principal aspects of her character, her passion for a person as yet unnamed and her inappropriately advanced age. On another level, typical of much theatrical monologue in the period, it does so in a relatively lyrical style. Closer examination of Marfilie's poetry reveals considerably more, however.

Perhaps the most obvious metaphorical reference in Marfilie's initial speech is her allusion to "un philtre nouveau," which "Ensorcelle mes sens." Described explicitly as a love potion, this "philtre" nevertheless has much in common with the poisons which sometimes appeared on the later seventeenth-century stage. Marfilie's "philtre" is also a "feu" that "rampe dans mon coeur." It is a "flame cruelle,/Furetans dans mes os," and which "consume leur moüelle." Elsewhere in the passage there is a reference, perhaps a little unusual even in the baroque-era theater, to "un foetide excrement" which Marfilie's "moite cerveau distille incessamment," as well as to a "chaude flame," to "feu" (twice), to "Enfer," and the verbs "eschauffer" and "embraser." The passage also offers some clear opposites, "les glaces," and Marfilie's former attractiveness even for those suitors who were "les plus froids."

These references are echoed frequently in the play, both before and after discussion of actual poison as it relates to the play's intrigue. Marfilie's nurse reminds her of those times when "en vos jeunes ans le poison aigre, doux/D'Amour petit sorcier empoisonnoit vostre ame" ["in your younger years the bittersweet poison of Love, that little sorcerer, poisoned your soul"] (p. 6). The servant Thomas, discoursing against love, declares that "J'ayme mieux m'enyvrer de la liqueur Bachique,/Que par ton fol poison devenir frenetique" ["I would rather drunk myself with Bacchic liquor than go wild with your insane poison"] (p. 27). And in act 5, the First Counselor discourses against "le venimeux poison/De la corruption" ["the venemous poison of corruption"] (p. 42).

In addition to numerous references to poison, fire, and unpleasant bodily fluids elsewhere in the text, the play's mythological references develop both the light and fire of the sun and the fire, darkness, and other unpleasant aspects of hell. Thus there are references to "Phoebus," to the "Oeil du Ciel," and to the "Oeil Latonien" (pp. 6, 21, 37). The play speaks of "Charon," of "Pluton," of Cerberus and "stigieux" darkness (pp. 14, 29, 31, 54). Auvray's personages refer to a variety of mythological fires and fiery things, for example the "Argoliques flames," Prometheus, and Mount Etna (pp. 23, 45, 48). Significantly, when Marfilie's son Anthoine drinks the sleeping potion, he feels not flames or heat, but cold: "Dieu! qu'il est savoureux! Mais quel froid me resserre/Les paupieres des yeux? quels pavots, quels glaçons/Causent dedans mes nerfs ces horribles frissons?" ["God! it is tasty! But what cold presses my eyelids to my eyes? What opium, what ice causes in my nerves these terrible shudders?"] (p. 39).

A second important metaphor announced in Marfilie's opening speech is that of beauty as opposed to ugliness or even monstrosity. Thus Marfilie complains that, in addition to her sufferings from the "foetide excrement," she now "courbe sous le poix/De mes ans escoulez." Her forehead is covered with "mainte noire ride." Marfilie laments further that "Mes jouës ne sont plus neigeusement pourprines./Et le Corail besson de mes levres sucrines/Palle ne semond plus un amoureux

baiser." Like her references to fire, cold, and poison, Marfilie's references to beauty and ugliness have numerous resonances elsewhere in the
play. In act 3, for example, Fabrice soliloquizes about earthly evils and
concludes that of all the obstacles to virtue, woman is the worst:

> La femme est le plus grand: ô perfide animal,
> Devois tu estre né pour faire tant de mal?
> O monstre envenimé, de tous malheurs l'extresme,
> Qui n'a rien de constant que l'inconstance mesme,
> Combien as-tu germé au monde de malheurs?

[Woman is the greatest: oh perfidious animal, need you have been
born to do so much evil? Oh, venemous monster, the extreme case
of all misfortunes, who has nothing constant but her very inconstance, how many worldly evils have you spawned?] (p. 23).

Fabrice mixes these notions of poison and monstrosity before hearing
Marfilie's declaration of love and before being accused of poisoning
Anthoine. Later, having heard Marfilie's declaration, Fabrice compares
her—in a reference which underlines the play's debt to the Phaedra
legend—to "ceste orde Pasiphaé, ceste Girce [for *garce?* for *Circé?*]
impudique" ["That foul Pasiphaé, that lewd bitch"]. Two lines later he
refers explicitly to her monstrous qualities as he apostrophizes the
Earth: "Pourquoy permettez-vous que ce monstre pervers/Presse si
longuement vos entrailles nourrices?" ["Why do you allow this perverse monster so long to compress your nurturing entrails?"] (p. 37). At
the play's denouement the judge castigates Marfilie as an "Implacable
furie" ["Implacable fury"] (p. 54) and a "monstre infernal" ["infernal
monster"] (p. 56). Such imprecations are echoed elsewhere, moreover,
by references to such other mythological monsters as Megaera, Hecate,
the already cited Cerberus, the monster-killer Hercules, and the non-
mythological but biblical story of Sampson and Delilah.

The reader may also speculate on the possible metaphorical implications of some other features of Marfilie's initial speech. In addition to
the verbs "ramper" and "furetans" and some color references, rather
rare in later dramatic poetry, Marfilie's monologue offers references to
things that come in twos—for example, the "Corail besson" or twin
coral of Marfilie's lips. This latter metaphorical suggestion is developed
by references to Scylla and Charybdis, the two counselors, and of
course Marfilie's two sons (e.g., pp. 6, 19, 32).

Considerably more important for the play as a whole, however, is a more general series of allusions in Marfilie's initial speech to the problem of disorder. Suggesting a kind of mental chaos, Marfilie laments that, in addition to losing her beauty, she has seen her mental powers diminish: "A grande peine ma voix," she cries, "Exprime les conceps de mon esprit languide." Her suggestion of conceptual disorder is echoed elsewhere in the text when she exhorts Thomas to "fay voir qu'à ton parler l'effet est tout conforme,/Le parler sans effect est un corps sans sa forme" ["show that the results conform to your words, for words without results are a body without form"] (p. 31). Reversing this suggestion as to the relative value of the abstract and the concrete, the First Counselor suggests in act 5 that the "appuy des loix va tousjours estayant/Des fragilles humains les commerces fragilles" ["the support of the laws still holds up the fragile affairs of fragile humans"] (p. 47).

The problem of disorder is cosmic as well as epistemological, as Marfilie's initial speech also suggests. In that introductory passage, love is evoked as possessing not only fire, wounds, bait, and nets but also is depicted as making war "au ciel et à l'Enfer, à l'air et à la terre." This reference is developed, varied, and amplified by the previously quoted references to the antipathies of the elements and to a possible return to a world of chaos, among other similar suggestions, until at the play's end this persistent disorder is resolved by the condemnation of Marfilie and her accomplices. On this occasion Fabrice thanks the ordering power of God, in a series of stanzas which cast in final form the principal metaphors of the play.

THE METAPHORICAL preoccupations of Auvray's play bear a remarkable similarity to those identified by Hubert in the *Phèdre* of the great Racine, almost as if the Phaedra legend in some sense lends itself to — or in some Jungian archetypal sense requires — exploitation of certain metaphorical possibilities. This is true both in the initial passage and throughout the later play, even though Racine's text begins not with a monologue by the heroine but with a conversation between Hippolyte and his *gouverneur* Théramène:

> HIPPOLYTE
> Le dessein en est pris: je pars, cher Théramène,
> Et quitte le séjour de l'aimable Trézène.
> Dans le doute mortel dont je suis agité,
> Je commence à rougir de mon oisiveté.

Depuis plus de six mois éloigné de mon père,
J'ignore le destin d'une tête si chère;
J'ignore jusqu'aux lieux qui le peuvent cacher.

THÉRAMÈNE

Et dans quels lieux, Seigneur, l'allez-vous donc chercher?
Déjà, pour satisfaire à votre juste crainte,
J'ai couru les deux mers que sépare Corinthe;
J'ai demandé Thésée aux peuples de ces bords
Où l'on voit l'Achéron se perdre chez les morts;
J'ai visité l'Elide, et laissant le Ténare,
Passé jusqu'à la mer qui vit tomber Icare.
Sur quel espoir nouveau, dans quels heureux climats
Croyez-vous découvrir la trace de ses pas?

[HIPPOLYTE

The decision is made: I go, dear Théramène, and leave the confines of pleasant Trézène. In the mortal doubt that upsets me, I begin to blush at my inactivity. Far from my father for more than six months, I do not know the destiny of so dear a person. I do not know even what place may hide him.

THÉRAMÈNE

And in what place, my Lord, will you go look for him? I have sailed the two seas that Corinth separates. I have asked after Theseus among the people of those borders where they see the Achéron descend into the land of the dead. I have visited the Elide and, leaving the Ténare, have passed over to the sea which saw Icarus's fall. Because of what new hope, in what happy climes do you think you will discover the traces of his steps?].[6]

This initial passage suggests the opposition between light and dark, between *locus amoenus* and hell already seen in Auvray's *L'Innocence descouverte*—and which Hubert finds developed and repeated throughout Racine's *Phèdre*. Thus Hippolyte speaks of "aimable Trézène" and Théramène of the "heureux climats," which may be harboring Theseus. Théramène speaks of the Achéron, that river which, according to legend, flows down into hell, that Achéron which will "se perdre chez les morts." Hippolyte, for his part, speaks of the "lieux" which may "cacher" his father. Elsewhere in the play, as Hubert points out, the pure light of the sun—Phaedra's ancestor—is contrasted not only with hell but also with the dark and confusing caverns of the labyrinth.

The beauty and ugliness of which Marfilie spoke in *L'Innocence descouverte* appear as the "tête si chère" of Theseus, later to be contrasted—again as Hubert points out—with monstrosity. Monstrosity, in Racine's play, takes the triple form of illicit passion, the Minotaur, and the sea dragon that finally brings about Hippolyte's death. Monsters and monstrousness appear, moreover, in a considerable variety of contexts. Indeed, in the lines immediately following the initial passage quoted, Théramène suggests that Theseus's incognito may be voluntary and that that notorious philanderer may even now be pursuing some new "amante abusée," a suggestion that Hippolyte immediately rejects as ... monstrous.

For Hubert, passion in *Phèdre* is not only illicit but also dehumanizing and denaturing, as if it were the work of a malicious, exterior force. As Hubert writes, "La passion, en jetant ses victimes dans un désordre extrême, détermine une espèce d'aliénation, dans le sens premier de ce mot: l'amoureux devient un autre ... " ["Passion, throwing its victims into extreme disorder, causes a sort of alienation, in the first sense of the word: the lover becomes a different person ... "]. It is in this sense—as well as in the more literal allusion to the "deux mers" that are separated by the peninsula of Corinth—that Racine's *Phèdre* develops the notion of things that come in twos, that is, in things separated. Hubert insists also on Racine's frequent use of the word "bords," a sign of separation and differentness, and one represented here in *Phèdre*'s initial passage.[7]

Racine's initial lines introduce also, and finally, the notion of disorder—if not chaos—that informed the earlier play. Thus Hippolyte speaks of his no doubt Jansenistic "doute mortel," of his agitation, and of his ignorance of some essential information. And Théramène echoes his expression of a "juste crainte." Théramène speaks also, in the lines immediately following, of the "mystère" of Theseus's whereabouts, a mystery developed and also elucidated throughout the play in conjunction with the notions of hell, separation, and the labyrinth.

All this is not to say, of course, that Jean Auvray's play has a profundity that it does not possess, nor that Auvray's text and Racine's, similar in the metaphors of their metaphorical unity, do not differ greatly and significantly. These differences are not merely a matter of differing poetic skill or poetic inspiration, moreover. To explain some of the differences it may be necessary to suggest, as Hubert himself has suggested, that metaphorical unity, too, has a history or a diachrony of its own.

Actually, in the sixteenth-century versions of the Phaedra legend, Garnier's and Yeuwain's, for example, metaphorical references are numerous and varied, as might befit expressions of any essentially analogical Renaissance worldview. Typically, metaphorical references in mid-sixteenth-century theater range over a very great many subjects drawn from the extensive repertoire of traditional poetry. In later sixteenth-century texts various distancing devices call attention to the metaphors as such—just as they did in the architectural sonnets cited in a previous chapter—thereby calling into question the function of metaphorical references as an adequate description of the world.

In Auvray's play, as analyzed here, the metaphorical range is extensive, and the mythological references are diffuse. These metaphors, however, group themselves into a relatively limited number of categories—so that they find their unity not in the full repertoire of the metaphorical system of the entire poetic world, but in a more limited system operative specifically inside the text itself—a metaphorical system of inner coherence. Each metaphorical category—fire, beauty, monstrosity, and so on—relates an aspect of the plot to the metaphorical universe of traditional poetry.

In Racine's play the nature of metaphorical coherence is strikingly different yet again. For instead of linking the action of the play to the metaphorical universe—the flowers or the elemental forces of nature—Racine relates both the play's action and metaphor to the different and relatively more conceptualized universe of Phaedra's "family history"—the legend of the Minotaur, the labyrinth, the abandonment of Ariane, and all the rest. Other versions of the Phaedra legend use similar metaphors—the sun, the dark regions of hell, the monster, and the labyrinth. However, as Hubert points out, Racine's work relates metaphorical elements to the action through a second, separate narrative, which forms a kind of key to the metaphorical understanding of the text.

Using a loose analogy, the difference between *L'Innocence descouverte* and Racine's *Phèdre* is like the difference between certain types of cryptographic messages. The simplest cryptograms are based on a principle of simple substitution: A becomes the number one, B becomes two, C becomes three, and so on. In a system of this kind, as indeed in the dream symbolism of ancient dream-explanation books, the relation of the symbol to its referent is fixed. In somewhat more sophisticated cryptographic systems, however—as indeed in the dream interpretations of Jung and Freud—the relation between symbol and referent is not fixed, but depends on the operation of a predetermined key. In the same way metaphors in Racine's *Phèdre* relate to the plot or to other play themes through a preselected key, the legend of Phaedra's ancestors or the legend of the Minotaur.

Operating in this way, the complex metaphorical unity of Racine's play may be said to be relatively more systematized, intellectualized, and rationalized than Garnier's or Auvray's. The same kind of difference—the distancing, reduction, simplification, and progressive intellectualization of metaphorical structure—may be observed in other texts from the same periods, between Montchrestien's *Aman* of 1601 (and 1604) and Racine's *Esther* of 1689, or between the already-cited Mellin de Saint-Gelais's or Montchrestien's or Mairet's *Sophonisbe's* of 1560, 1596 (and 1601 and 1604), and 1634, respectively, and the later *Sophonisbe* of Corneille (1663). Or between Corneille's *Médée* of 1635 and Longepierre's 1694 version of the same legend.

The last example may merit slightly more detailed analysis. In Corneille's earlier version the dress that Medea sends to her rival Créuse, a dress which subsequently will burn Créuse to death on stage, is on consensus, a baroque dress. Créuse exclaims:

> Qu'elle a fait un beau choix! jamais éclat pareil
> Ne sema dans la nuit les clartés du soleil;
> Les perles avec l'or confusément mêlées,
> Mille pierres de prix sur ses bords étalées,
> D'un mélange divin éblouissent les yeux;
> Jamais rien d'approchant ne se fit en ces lieux.

[What a beautiful choice she made! No like brilliance ever sowed into the night the shimmers of the sun; gold confusingly mixed with pearls, a thousand precious stones laid out upon the edges dazzle the eyes with a divine mixture; nothing remotely like this was ever made in this place].[8]

The dress in Longepierre's play, as described by Medea herself, is somewhat different:

Rhodope, tu connois cette robe éclattante
Du rubis lumineuse et d'or étincellante;
Parure inestimable, ornement precieux
Où l'art et la richesse éblouissent les yeux.
Le Soleil, mon ayeul, favorisant mon Pere,
Pour present nuptial en fit don à ma Mere;
Et semble avoir mêlé pour enrichir ses dons
Le feu de sa lumiere à l'or de ses rayons.
C'est de tous les tresors où je pouvois pretendre,
L'unique qu'en fuyant Médée ait daigné prendre.
Tu sçais qu'en arrivant en ces funestes lieux,
De Créüse éblouie elle enchanta les yeux.
Admirant son éclat et vantant sa richesse,
Elle a tout employé, pierres, dons, promesse,
Pour pouvoir posseder ce superbe ornement.
Il faut qu'à ma vengeance il serve d'instrument.
Je vais l'empoisonner, et par mon art funeste
Mêler un prompt venin à son éclat celeste;
Mille sucs empestez, mille charmes divers;
Et la Rage, et la Mort, et l'horreur des enfers.

[Rhodope, do you know that robe embroidered with luminous rubies and sparkling gold; priceless garment, precious ornament in which art and riches dazzle the eyes. The Sun, my grandfather, honoring my father, gave it as a wedding present to my mother; he seems to have mixed in it, to make a richer gift, the fire of his light and the gold of his rays. It is, of all the treasures to which I might pretend, the only one that Medea, as she fled, deigned to take. You know how, as we arrived in these fatal places, it enchanted the dazzled Créuse. Admiring its glitter and praising its richness, she tried all means, stones, gifts, promises, in order to possess this superb ornament. It must serve as the instrument of my vengeance. I shall poison it, and by my fatal art mix a quick venom with its celestial light; a thousand plague essences, a thousand various charms; and rage, and death, and the horrors of hell].[9]

Now in each case Medea's robe is a magnificent art object. In both versions, moreover, that object is ornamented with things which come by the thousands, whether "sucs empestez," "charmes divers," or "pierres de prix." In both versions, also, the garment's many ornaments dazzle the eyes. However, in Longepierre's version, the possibly baroque suggestions of "éclat" and "mélange" are partly replaced by appeals to sentiment. The possibly baroque commonplace that compares the robe's dazzling brilliance to the sparks of the sun—and hence the products of art to the beauties of nature—is replaced, in Longepierre's text, by a relatively superficial, possibly rococo comparison of "l'art et la richesse."

As for the attitudes toward cognition in the two plays, Corneille's *Médée* begins with appeals to curiously naïve sentiment:

POLLUX

Que je sens à la fois de surprise et de joie!
Se peut-il qu'en ces lieux enfin je vous revoie,
Que Pollux dans Corinthe ait rencontré Jason?

JASON

Vous n'y pouviez venir en meilleure saison;
Et pour vous rendre encor l'âme plus étonnée,
Préparez-vous à voir mon second hyménée.

POLLUX

Quoi! Médée est donc morte, ami?

JASON

Non, elle vit;
Mais un objet plus beau la chasse de mon lit.

[POLLUX

How surprised I am, and at once how joyful! Can it be that I may see you again here, after so long, that Pollux in Corinth has met again with Jason?

JASON

You couldn't be coming in a better season; and to astonish your soul even more, prepare yourself to see my second wedding.

POLLUX

What? Is Medea then dead, my friend?

JASON

No, she lives; but a more beautiful person replaces her in my bed.][10]

Longepierre's play begins, on the contrary, with a discussion of legal or moral rights and ideas:

Je sçais ce que je dois à l'amour de Medée.
Cesse, Iphite, à mes yeux d'en retracer l'idée.
Ce qu'elle a fait pour moi, dans la Grece, à Colchos,
Ne traverse que trop ma joye et mon repos.

[I know what I owe to the love of Medea. Iphite, cease retracing that idea before my eyes. What she did for me, in Greece, at Colchos, spoils only too much my joy and my repose].

Whereas much of seventeenth-century French literature concerned choices between love and duty, between finesse and geometry, between heart and reason—and hence between an *épistémè* of resemblance and one of representation—in Longepierre's play these seemingly eternal dichotomies seem strangely to have been resolved. Personages choose not between resemblance and reason but between alternatives presented within the context of representational thought. When questioned on the issue of love and reason by Iphite, Jason answers: "Non, la raison ici d'accord avec mon coeur,/Autorise ma flâme et soûtient mon ardeur" ["No, here reason, in accord with my heart, authorizes my love and sustains my ardor"]. Elsewhere in the play, Medea declares that "l'amour et la raison ont vaincu ma fureur" ["love and reason have vanquished my furor"].[11]

Typically the seventeenth-century works presented in this and previous chapters have presented coexistence, confrontation, and conflict between competing *épistémès* and arranged, in their conclusions, some kind of synthesis between them—something like the previously quoted "accord momentané entre une faculté de sentir et une faculté de penser" suggested by Henri Peyre as the essence of the classical aesthetic. In the last decades of the seventeenth century, however, the sources of epistemological uncertainty and competition that are thus, perhaps, at the heart of French classicism in the *Grand Siècle* may have had less interest for authors, spectators, and readers—insofar as any dramatic conflict took place within a realm of representation. In Foucaldian terms such a transformation should represent the casting out of folly—and any truly tragic horror and pity—from a universe of representation and rationalism. In terms used by Kuhn, satisfying assimilation of the paradigm of representation might permit something like a return to "normal literature," that is, literature which explored the consequences of a single, unified model of truth. As a result, kingly authority, which in Cornelian times resolved irreconcilable difficulties, appears in

Longepierre either as a tranquil, integrated, rational function — or as its opposite, the tyrannical, arbitrary exercise of power. In either case, whether in Longepierre's *Médée* or Racine's *Athalie,* kingly authority appears as the guardian of a world in which epistemological issues have essentially been resolved.

N O T E S

1. Garnier, *Oeuvres complètes,* 2 (Paris: Garnier, 1923), pp. 239–341; Yeuwain, *Hippolyte* (Mons: L. Dequesne, 1933); La Pinelière, *Hippolyte* (Paris, 1635); Gilbert, *Hypolite ou le garçon insensible* (Paris, 1647). References in text are hereafter given as author, page number(s).

These and other French versions of the Phaedra legend are studied in Claude Francis's helpful *Les Métamorphoses de Phèdre dans la littérature française* (Quebec: Pélican, 1967).

2. Hubert, *Essai d'exégèse racinienne* (Paris: Nizet, 1956), p. 11. Concerning metaphorical unity, see also Hubert's *Molière and the Comedy of Intellect* (Berkeley: University of California Press, 1962); David Lee Rubin, *Higher Hidden Order: Design and Meaning in the Odes of Malherbe* (Chapel Hill: University of North Carolina Press, 1972); Reiss, *Toward Dramatic Illusion,* and, in a Foucaldian vein, the same author's *Tragedy and Truth* (New Haven: Yale University Press, 1980); W. B. Kay, *The Theatre of Jean Mairet: The Metamorphosis of Sensuality* (The Hague: Mouton, 1975). A recent collective volume edited by Van Baelen and Rubin brings together essays under the title *La Cohérence intérieure.*

3. Although confusion about the identity of Auvray has seemingly been definitely resolved (see Adam, *Histoire de la littérature française,* 1: 74), the bibliography of his Phaedra play remains obscure. Descriptions of the first edition (on consensus, Auvray, *Marfilie* [Rouen: J. Petit, 1609]) vary. That first edition is, moreover, *rarissime* today. Although copies are listed in old catalogues, circularization by interlibrary loan services suggests that no copy survives in any public collection in France or the United States. To my knowledge, no twentieth-century source offers commentary clearly based on the first edition. The edition of 1628 (included in Auvray's *Banquet des muses* [Rouen: J. Petit, 1628]) is easier to find and seems likely to be the basis of the small body of twentieth-century critical description.

The situation points up once again the problems encountered by anyone who wishes to take seventeenth-century diachrony seriously. In the absence of any copy of the first edition, the empiricist may well wonder whether he is studying a text from 1609 or 1628, a question this chapter does not attempt to answer. Some comfort is offered, however, by an eighteenth-century commentator, the Abbé Goujet. In his *Bibliothèque française* (Paris, 1740–56), he writes that it is not true, as some have asserted, that the 1609 and 1628 versions are different: "J'ai comparé les deux Piéces; elles sont les mêmes" ["I have compared the two plays; they are the same"] (15: 319–20). See also L. E. Dabney, *French Dramatic Literature in the Reign of Henri IV* (Austin: University Cooperative Society, 1952).

4. Lancaster, *History of French Dramatic Literature in the Seventeenth Century* (Baltimore: Johns Hopkins University Press, 1929), 1:24. See also Lancaster, "Alexandre Hardy et ses rivaux," *RHL* 24 (1917), 414–21. Dabney gives *The Golden Ass* rather than Seneca or Euripides as the play's principal source, although, he says, "The author also keeps the Seneca (or Garnier) version of the Phaedra story constantly in mind . . ." (*French Dramatic Literature*, p. 220).

5. Auvray, *L'Innocence descouverte*, in *Banquet des muses*, p. 26. Henceforth references are given in the text.

6. In Racine, *Théâtre complet* (Paris: Garnier, 1960), pp. 543, 548 (act 1, scenes 1 and 3).

7. Hubert, *Essai d'exégèse racinienne*, p. 203.

8. In *Théâtre complet* (Paris: Garnier, n.d.), 1: 465; 2: 4.

9. Longpierre, *Médée* (Paris: Nizet: 1967), pp. 80–81 (act 3, scene 4).

10. Corneille, *Théâtre complet*, 1: 447 (act 1, scene 1).

11. Longepierre, *Médée*, pp. 33–34, 75 (act 1, scene 1; act 3, scene 3).

CHAPTER 10

Two Fables Attacking Superstition: La Fontaine's *Astrologue* and *Animal dans la lune*

THE LITERARY CAREER of La Fontaine was a long one, stretching from the 1650s through his period of greatest acclaim as a raconteur and fabulist in the 1660s and 1670s and continuing into the 1690s, a rather different age. A literal-minded, chronological study of La Fontaine would show, moreover, a striking evolution in the poet's taste through the decades. One suggestive example is two treatments by La Fontaine of a subject present in literature at least since the sixteenth century, the evils of unscientific superstition. These are La Fontaine's *L'Astrologue qui se laisse tomber dans un puits,* first published in Book Two of the *Fables* in 1668, and *Un Animal dans la lune,* written perhaps a year before the peace of Nimègue, in 1677.[1]

In contrast with Ronsard or Jean Auvray or Honoré d'Urfé or Thibault or Schélandre or even the author of *Le Cid* or Pascal, both poems take a clear-cut position favoring what would today be considered scientific knowledge over knowledge gained by relatively intuitive means. In the *Astrologue* La Fontaine's universe is essentially regular, impersonal, and astronomical. In a poetic statement constituting—and indeed perhaps more or less consciously intended to be—a denial of the system of resemblance, sympathy, and emulation, La Fontaine evokes the firmament which "se meut," and in which "les astres font leur cours, /Le soleil nous luit tous les jours" ["moves" and in which "the stars prescribe their course, the sun shines down every day"] and reiterates:

> Tous les jours sa clarté succède à l'ombre noire,
> Sans que nous en puissions autre chose inférer
> Que la nécessité de luire et d'éclairer,
> D'amener les saisons, de mûrir les semences,
> De verser sur les corps certaines influences.
> Du reste, en quoi répond au sort toujours divers
> Ce train toujours égal dont marche l'univers?

[Every day its light follows the black shadow, without our being able to infer anything but the necessity to shine and light, to bring the seasons, to ripen seeds, to shed on bodies certain influences. As for the rest, in what way may the always regular movement of the universe be related to always varying fate?]

In developments suggesting Michel Foucault's description of the exclusion of folly from the world of normal discourse, La Fontaine attacks necromancers and soothsayers, "Charlatans, faiseurs d'horoscopes" ["charlatans, horoscope casters"], "souffleurs" ["puffers"], and all those who "ne méritez pas plus de foi que ces gens" ["merit no more faith than they"], as well as anyone credulous enough to believe in their nonsense. La Fontaine writes, in this poem of the 1660s, that "Il en est peu qui fort souvent/Ne se plaisent d'entendre dire/Qu'au livre du Destin les mortels peuvent lire" ["There are few who most often are displeased to hear it said that mortals may read in the book of destiny"]. Any such book represents for La Fontaine that wisdom which the late sixteenth-century celebrated as specifically poetic knowledge. The book of destiny is the one which "Homère et les siens ont chanté" ["Homer and his tribe have sung"]. However, La Fontaine's concluding moral makes even the astrologer himself not the privileged seer of an earlier view but the "image de ceux qui baîllent aux chimères" ["image of those who are thunderstruck by illusions"]. In the *Astrologue* poetic or intuitive knowledge becomes chance, "le hasard." As such, for La Fontaine, it falls outside the domain of those things which are appropriate objects of knowledge. As he writes, "du hasard il n'est point de science./S'il en était, on auroit tort/De l'appeler hasard, ni fortune, ni sort,/Toutes choses très incertaines" ["For chance, there is no science. If there were one, it would be wrong to call it chance, or fortune, or destiny—all most uncertain things"].

Any such attack on poetic knowledge as superstition notwithstanding, in his *Astrologue* La Fontaine continues to describe human uncertainties and elemental forces in traditional poetic terms. In the passage quoted above, sun and shadow, the crops and the seasons are described in terms understandable to Ronsard or Malherbe, even as La Fontaine uses them for other purposes. Elsewhere in the fable, God, the night, and the stars are personified and humanized in a presumably ironic mock-baroque evocation. Who knows the secrets of destiny, La Fontaine asks, "que lui seul? Comment lire en son sein?/Aurait-il imprimé sur le front des étoiles/Ce que la nuit des temps enferme dans ses voiles?" ["but He alone? How might one read in His bosom? Would He have printed on the forehead of the stars that which the night of time encloses in its veils?"]

Such metaphorical or intuitive evocations are echoed, moreover, in the underlying structure of the fable. Although much shorter, of course, than any five-act play, La Fontaine's *Astrologue* benefits from the inner coherence or metaphorical unity studied previously in seventeenth-century—and particularly Racinian—theater. Like those of earlier plays generally, the metaphorical unity of the *Astrologue* depends essentially on certain "elemental" notions of traditional poetry. Some of these become apparent even in the poem's first four lines:

> Un astrologue un jour se laissa choir
> Au fond d'un puits. On lui dit: "Pauvre bête,
> Tandis qu'à peine à tes pieds tu peux voir,
> Penses-tu lire au-dessus de ta tête?"

[One day an astrologer made the mistake of falling to the bottom of a well. Someone said to him: "Poor beast, how do you hope to read above your head, when you can hardly see down to your feet?].

Proceeding more or less mechanically to seek repetitions of words or categories of words, these lines offer at least two expressions of temporality: "un jour" and "tandis que." There are also several expressions of verticality: "choir," "Au fond," "puits," "Pauvre"—an expression of low status—"pieds," and, of course, "au-dessus de ta tête." One might wish to add La Fontaine's reference to the "astrologue," since it forms one element of a social hierarchy at the other end of which is the "Pauvre bête," also referred to. As in all the works studied up to this point, there are references to the modes of volition and cognition. Thus the astrologer "se laissa choir" and "peu[t] voir." A bystander asks him if he "pense[ ] . . . lire" over his head.

Whether most essentially Hubertian "metaphors" or Greimasian "modalities," these repeated types of expression have resonances elsewhere in the poem. The notion of verticality, associated with social status and value, appears in further references to the intellectual standing of astrologers and the relationship between man and God. There is further reference to classical antiquity and the sublime poet Homer—another true authority—in contrast to the false authority of astrologers. Still later in the poem the "Charlatans, faiseurs d'horoscope," and "souffleurs" are contrasted with their betters, the "princes de l'Europe." The author himself is depicted as subject to exaggeration: "Je m'emporte un peu trop; revenons à l'histoire . . . " ["I'm getting a little carried away; let's return to the story . . . "].

The notion of relative value has other echoes in the poem. Just as the false science, the "art mensonger" of the astrologers contrasts with the true science of Providence, so the singular and unrepeatable effects of contingency are contrasted with the general, regular, and predictable events of a universe governed by natural law. In the service of this notion the initial temporal references to "un jour" and "tandis que" stand in contrast to the "train toujours égal dont marche l'univers." Those persons who, "fort souvent," are so ill advised as to attempt to predict the future are opposites of God who, "lui seul," knows the future's secrets. The antiscience of chance balances the "nécessité de luire et d'éclairer." In the concluding moral La Fontaine again creates contrast between those who "baîllent aux chimères" and the possibility of danger to themselves or, as a last evocation of relative value, their "affaires."

IN 1677 LA FONTAINE'S *Un Animal dans la lune* again attacks superstition, but in a somewhat different manner and within a differently structured metaphorical context. Like many of La Fontaine's later *contes* and fables, tending perhaps to a more rococo treatment of its subject, *Un Animal dans la lune* is longer and structurally more complex than the *Astrologue*. In the first fourteen lines of the *Animal*, La Fontaine poses a well-known philosophical—or scientific—problem, that of the accuracy of sense perception. The opening formula, "Pendant qu'un philosophe assure . . . Un autre philosophe jure" ["Whereas one philosopher asserts (that) . . . Another philosopher swears (that)"], introduces two alternative bodies of seventeenth-century thought on the subject. The first, rooted in something like the *épistémè* of resemblance and its subsequent "crisis," suggests that sense perception is fundamentally "correct," a direct access to a directly comprehensible world. The second view, a kind of "crisis" reaction to the first, suggests that, in the light of various well-known paradoxes of sense perception, sense perception is fundamentally "incorrect."

In a second part of the poem La Fontaine gives examples of problems of sense perception—the stick apparently bent as it is viewed through water, the apparent as compared to the real size of the solar disc, and the like. The author's conclusion, clearly putting to good use the epistemology of classification, is a synthesis of the two hypotheses. As La Fontaine writes:

Tous les deux ont raison: et la philosophie
Dit vrai, quand elle dit que les sens tromperont
Tant que sur leur rapport les hommes jugeront;
  Mais aussi, si l'on rectifie
L'image de l'objet sur son éloignement,
  Sur le milieu qui l'environne,
  Sur l'organe et sur l'instrument,
  Les sens ne tromperont personne.
La nature ordonna ces choses sagement.

[Both are right: and philosophy is correct to say that the senses deceive, as long as men judge them at face value; but also, if one rectifies the image of an object according to its distance, to the medium that surrounds it, to the organ and the instrument, the senses will deceive no one. Nature ordained these things wisely].

In an early example of what has been called the "rhetoric of science" in literature, La Fontaine adds, pedantically or pseudopedantically, "J'en dirai quelque jour les raisons amplement" ["I will someday expound the reasons more amply"].

A third part of the poem recounts a kind of fable, ostensibly related to the preceding discussion. Adapted from Samuel Butler's "The Elephant in the Moon," it tells how amazing monsters seemingly discovered on the moon turn out to be a mouse trapped in the observer's telescope. In the *Animal*, just as La Fontaine suggested also in the *Astrologue*, it is the king of England himself who puts to rest popular hysteria by examining the telescope and finding the mouse. Next, a fourth part of the fable, apparently departing abruptly from the first, second, and third, exhorts the French to end their current wars and reap the benefits of peace. These benefits are enjoyed by British subjects, and La Fontaine suggests that Louis XIV might benefit, like Charles of England, from some of the fruits of peaceful civilization.

Thus treating rather diverse subjects in a single poem, La Fontaine's *Animal* offers principally not a choice between magic and science, or between resemblance and classification as was the case in the *Astrologue*, but instead a choice between two explanations, presumably equally scientific, of a philosophical question. The synthetic solution offered mixes not poetic and classificatory modes, but rather two modes of classification. In another sense, moreover, La Fontaine proposes less a choice between two types of classification—there may be only one true rational solution, after all—but rather simply a choice between truth and error. La Fontaine's view of truth depends on the notion of levels of classification—perception as corrected by various levels of conceptualization. Speaking of the apparent size of the sun, La Fontaine addresses an illusion which is independent of the poetic worldview: "J'aperçois le soleil: quelle en est la figure?/Ici-bas ce grand corps n'a que trois pieds de tour. . . . Sa distance me fait juger de sa grandeur . . . " ["I perceive the sun; what is its image? Here below this great body is only three feet in circumference. . . . (correction for) its distance makes me judge (correctly) its size . . . "]. Continuing, La Fontaine distinguishes between "L'ignorant" who "le croit plat" ["The ignorant man" who "believes it flat"] and the reasonable man, in the occurrence La Fontaine himself:

> . . . j'épaissis sa rondeur;
> Je le rends immobile, et la terre chemine.
> Bref je demens mes yeux en toute sa machine.
> Ce sens ne me nuit point par son illusion.

[. . . I thicken its roundness; I make it immobile, and the earth moves. In brief, I refute my eyes as to all of its aspects. This sense in no way confounds me with its illusion.]

Drawing a very general conclusion, La Fontaine writes:

> Je ne suis point d'intelligence
> Avecque mes regards peut-être un peu trop prompts,
> Ni mon oreille lente à m'apporter les sons.
> Quand l'eau courbe un bâton, ma raison le redresse:

[I am not in collusion with my glances, perhaps a bit too quick, nor with my ear, slow to bring me sounds. When the water curves a stick, my reason straightens it back].

La Fontaine ends very generally indeed, in a sentence which looks ahead to the rationalism of the eighteenth century: "La raison," he writes, "décide en maîtresse" ["reason . . . decides as a mistress"].

If reason is the mistress, an overriding rather than a co-equal or complementary form of knowledge, one might wonder what becomes of poetic knowledge and expression in the later poem. Certainly La Fontaine retains much of the repertoire of "poetic" language and rhetoric. He writes, for example, that the sun, apparently only three feet in circumference when observed from the Earth, might be quite different if viewed from high in the sky. From there, he asks—falling back on a metaphor chosen in the traditional repertoire—"Que serait-ce à mes yeux que l'oeil de la Nature?" ["How would the eye of Nature appear to my eyes?"]. La Fontaine's earlier *Clymène* predicted an eventual decline of poetry, an age when the universe "Ne se souciera plus ni d'auteurs ni de vers" ["Will care no longer for authors nor for verse"] and when, as Apollo remarks to his muses, "vos divinités périront, et la mienne" ["your divinities will perish along with mine"].[2] But in *Un Animal dans la lune,* speaking of the benefits of peace for the French, La Fontaine returns nevertheless to some of the commonplaces of traditional poetry and official rhetoric:

> Mars nous fait recueillir d'amples moissons de gloire:
> C'est à nos ennemis de craindre les combats,
> A nous de les chercher, certains que la Victoire,
> Amante de Louis, suivra partout ses pas.
> Ses lauriers nous rendront célèbres dans l'histoire.
>   Même les filles de Mémoire
> Ne nous ont pas quittés; nous goûtons des plaisirs;
> La paix fait nos souhaits et non point nous soupirs.

[Mars helps us reap ample harvest of glory: it is for our enemies to fear combat, and for us to seek it, certain that Victory, Louis's mistress, will everywhere follow his lead. His laurels will make us famous in history. Even the daughters of memory have not forsaken us; we taste pleasures; peace is our wish and not our despair].

In similar fashion the narrative structure of *Un Animal dans la lune* subordinates its parts less to the whole even than La Fontaine's earlier *Astrologue.* While the *Astrologue*'s fable-story is overshadowed by a lengthy digression, the *Animal*'s last two parts are related only tenuously —whether in plot or in subject matter—to the first two. The last lines of the *Astrologue* return to the poem's principal subject, closing the circle of the plot in a traditional manner, while the structure of the *Animal* may have most in common with the "fractured fables" or deliberately deplotted stories of a much later age. Possibly rococo in its decentered structure, the *Animal* begins with philosophers, shifts to astronomers, crowds, and the king of England, and ends with the French and English people and the French and English kings—while nevertheless occasionally using some narrative elements of a traditional or Proppian or Greimasian kind within its various, very disparate parts.

In the same way finally, the poetic technique of metaphorical unity reappears—used somewhat differently—in La Fontaine's later poem. La Fontaine begins:

> Pendant qu'un philosophe assure
> Que toujours par leurs sens les hommes sont dupés,
>   Un autre philosophe jure
>   Qu'ils ne nous ont jamais trompés.
> Tous les deux ont raison: et la philosophie
> Dit vrai, quand elle dit que les sens tromperont
> Tant que sur leur rapport les hommes jugeront;
>   Mais aussi, si l'on rectifie
> L'image de l'objet sur son éloignement,
>   Sur le milieu qui l'environne,
>   Sur l'organe et sur l'instrument
>   Les sens ne tromperont personne.
> La nature ordonna ces choses sagement:
> J'en dirai quelque jour les raisons amplement.

[While one philosopher assures that men are always duped by their senses, another swears that they have never deceived us. Both are right . . . (see p. 138)].

Perhaps strikingly, a number of terms in the opening passage quoted above, while they may effectively express the underlying structure or cognitive dimension of the poem, are not metaphorical and do not contribute to any possibly metaphorical structure. Thus the philosophers are simply philosophers, spokesmen for the two points of view expressed in the poem. Other terms have unity simply because they fit into logical categories. These are the distance ["éloignement"], the organ ["organe"], the instrument, and the medium or milieu. All of these are related simply because they are various dimensions of perception, various sources of error needing to be rectified ["si l'on rectifie"] by intellectual operations. Some of these terms have echoes in the second section of the poem (for example, the distance within the telescope or the distance to the moon). It is not clear, however, that these rectificatory factors have close equivalents in the poem's final section.

La Fontaine's *Animal* is closer to his *Astrologue*'s style of metaphorical unity when it uses terms of binary opposition: "un," "autre," "aussi," "tous les deux," and "Pendant que" and "tant que." These terms, of course, correspond metaphorically to the opposition of the two philosophers and their two approaches to sense perception, to the two possible explanations of the monster in the telescope, and to the possibly opposing views of the kings of France and England concerning war and peace. In a more general sense all parts of the poem pose problems involving two conflicting views and, in para-Cornelian fashion, resolve them by appealing to some wise counsel. In the first two parts it is the voice of La Fontaine which affirms that "tous les deux ont raison." In the third part it is the king of England who "favorise en roi ces hautes connoissances" ["as king takes an interest in this lofty knowledge"] and who discovers the truth and dispels the error of his countrymen. In the fourth part La Fontaine expresses the hope that France will embrace the view already held in England. If this happens, the French "Auguste" —prince of peace—will be no less admirable than that other Caesar— "le premier des Césars"—was heroic in war.

In La Fontaine's *Un Animal dans la lune,* comparison of things perhaps not readily comparable—philosophies of perception and policies toward peace, mice, monsters, and the like—may be seen as a kind of poetic or intellectual exuberance or virtuosity, or indeed as that increase in metaphorical "distance" thought by some to be characteristic of the later stages of any given poetic movement. As such, it may suggest something like the imminent decline of poetry or of classicism—a traditional view. Or it may be seen as an expression of some emerging frivolity of the following, rococo age. Or as one more expression of some forthcoming Age of Reason. In any case, in a different manner than the oxymoron or *métaphore filée* associated with possibly baroque poetry, it depends essentially on intellectualizing certain salient characteristics of the objects compared. La Fontaine's later poem retains at the same time, however, some of the traditional poetic language, the traditional narrative motifs, and certain unifying *métaphores* in the Hubertian sense, as it posits a philosophical or scientific situation in which "la raison décide en maîtresse."[3]

As is well known, La Fontaine treated scientific and philosophical subjects frequently in later poems like his *Poème du Quinquina* of 1679–81 or his *Discours à Madame de la Sablière* of 1684. In the dedication of his twelfth and last book of fables, La Fontaine wrote in 1694 that "Nous n'avons plus besoin de consulter ni Apollon ni les Muses, ni aucune des divinités du Parnasse" ["We no longer need to consult Apollo or the muses, nor any other divinity of the Parnassus"]—a declaration which fulfills the prophecy of *Clymène* and belies the conclusion of *Un Animal dans la lune.* Addressing the duke of Burgundy, La Fontaine writes that these divinities "se rencontrent toutes dans les présents que vous a faits la nature, et dans cette science de bien juger des ouvrages de l'esprit, à quoi vous joignez déjà celle de connaître toutes les régles qui y conviennent" ["can all be found in the gifts which Nature has given you, and in that science of properly judging the works of the mind, to which you join that of knowing all the rules which are appropriate"]. To this suggestion that art will henceforth triumph over divinity, La Fontaine adds the simple affirmation, in the first fable of Book Twelve, that in the duke of Burgundy's court, "Le sens et la raison y réglent toute chose" ["Judgment and reason regulate everything"].[4]

LA FONTAINE'S INTEREST in both fables and scientific poetry was continued in the following decades by such poets as Lebrun-Pindare, Malfilâtre, Delille, and indeed Chénier. In his *Fables* of 1719 an avowed adversary of poetry, Antoine Houdart de la Motte, again took up the subject of La Fontaine's *Astrologue* and *Animal* and attacked superstition from a yet more comfortable distance than La Fontaine. In so doing he confirmed—like the later La Fontaine himself—a striking observation of Kuhn concerning the aftermath of scientific or other intellectual "revolutions." Kuhn writes that

> . . . changes of this sort are never total. Whatever he may then see, the scientist after a revolution is still looking at the same world. Furthermore, though he may previously have employed them differently, much of his language and most of his laboratory instruments are still the same as they were before. As a result, postrevolutionary science invariably includes many of the same manipulations, performed with the same instruments and described in the same terms, as its prerevolutionary predecessor. If these enduring manipulations have been changed at all, the change must lie either in their relation to the paradigm or in their concrete results.[5]

This remark might be applied rather generally to the poetry, to the theater, and to some other areas of intellectual endeavor in some emerging rococo age or some emerging Age of Reason.

N O T E S

1. La Fontaine, *Fables,* in *Oeuvres complètes* (Paris: Seuil, 1965), II, 13; VII, 18.

2. La Fontaine, *Oeuvres diverses* (Paris: Pléiade, 1948), p. 34.

3. J. D. Hubert, "Malherbe à l'assaut du Parnasse," *ECr* 16 (1976), 105. See also O. de Mourgues, *O Muse, fuyante proie* (Paris: Corti, 1962), pp. 183–86.

For further discussion of the unity of *Un Animal dans la lune,* see L. Spitzer, "Die Kunst des Ubergangs bei La Fontaine," *PMLA* 53 (1938), 393–433. Beverly S. Ridgely compares these two poems as episodes in the history of science in "Astrology and Astronomy in the *Fables* of La Fontaine," ibid., 80 (1965), 180–89. For the *épistémè(s)* of La Fontaine, see Michel Serres, "Le Jeu du Loup," in *Savoir, faire espérer* (Brussels: Fac. St. Louis, 1976).

4. La Fontaine, *Fables,* XII, ded., 1.

5. Kuhn, *Structure,* pp. 129–30.

CHAPTER 11

Conclusions

EMPIRICALLY APPLYING diverse methods, the textual comparisons in the preceding pages offer a variety of insights into the period between 1557 and 1719. Comparison of Du Bellay's description of Anet and Ronsard's description of Saint‑Cosme not only reveals the expected, more or less pronounced consensus mannerist or baroque qualities of each, but also places these qualities in a special perspective, that of increasing epistemological preoccupation. In this perspective, these qualities may reasonably be interpreted as movement toward some remarkable epistemological upheaval like Foucaldian epistemic change or Kuhnian awareness of crisis.

Awareness of some such crisis is clearly visible, moreover, in comparison of Montaigne (1580 and 1588) and Charron (*De la sagesse,* 1596 or 1601). Both texts are gloomy about the thought process, presenting multitudes of presumably baroque images of conflicting and inconclusive thinking, as well as a critique of most forms of human knowledge. The most striking difference between the two texts, however, is Charron's suggestion that through judicious choice the number of necessary factors may be reduced to some usable number. This practical approach presages Descartes's *Regulae* and *Discours de la méthode*—and the proposal of alternative solutions that, according to Kuhn, characterises a second stage of intellectual Gestalt shift.

Comparison of two texts from *L'Astrée* (1607 and 1610, respectively) finds two alternative epistemologies (or *épistémès*) coexisting and commingling, something like Renaissance analogical thinking or Foucaldian resemblance with something like Foucaldian representation, a reducing, ordering, classifying, and hierarchizing mode of knowledge further presaging what would later be seen as the Baconian or Cartesian revolution in science and philosophy. As such the epistemological preoccupations of *L'Astrée* are very similar to those of Cervantes's almost exactly contemporary Don Quixote as described in Foucault's

Les Mots et les choses. Moreover, *L'Astrée* contains so many epistemological statements of what were later described as Cornelian, or Precious or even Jansenist kinds that it suggests less a historical influence than a very general intellectual transformation.

Comparison of two perhaps unlikely texts—Saint-Didier's *Traicté* and Thibault's *Académie* on fencing (1583 and 1628)—suggests that similar transformations from relatively organic to relatively mathematized approaches occurred in at least one other domain at about the same period—subject nevertheless to working out according to specific, locally applicable conditions in somewhat the way suggested by Deleuze as he sought to refine the Foucaldian model in *Un Nouvel Archiviste.* Meanwhile, comparison of the 1608 and 1628 versions of Schélandre's obscure but fascinating *Tyr et Sidon* shows that while both versions share consensus mannerist or baroque elements, Cartesian or representational elements, the second is paradoxically "more baroque," using its analogical elements in a more conscious and deliberate-appearing manner, but also goes further toward attempting synthesis or some sort of Kuhnian tinkering with the two modes. Such a result goes some distance toward resolving the multiplicity and apparent inconclusiveness of definitions of mannerist and baroque styles proposed heretofore.

It might also deal effectively with the pseudoproblem of the coexistence of baroque and classicist preoccupations in much of the literature of the period. The tinkerer's synthesis of *Tyr et Sidon* is, of course, only one of a variety of possible reactions to a new paradigm of literary and intellectual understanding. Thus the following chapter's comparison of Garnier's *Bradamante* of 1582 with Corneille's *Le Cid* of 1636–37 suggests other possibilities—in particular a synthesis based on the legalistic notions symbolized in the later text by Cornelian *amour-estime* and the all-too-well-known conflicts of *amour* and *devoir,* as well as that "temps, ta vaillance, et ton Roi" which allow people to get through irreconcilable contradictions. In such a context the very rich Cornelian repertoire of forms of *bricolage* and epistemological leaping and "méthode de prudence" ["prudent method"] solutions appear as characteristic features—rather than anomalous weaknesses—of literature of the classical period.

In addition, comparison of a Cartesian mathematical proof with a similar one by Guillaume de l'Hospital (1637 and 1696) suggests that the priority in use of one or another aspect of the calculus is perhaps less important than the difference between Kuhnian "new" science and

Kuhnian "normal" science in the earlier and later decades of the seventeenth century. If Cartesian mathematics is in some sense Cornelian, and vice versa, then Newton and Leibniz, who are precisely the contemporaries of Boileau, La Fontaine, La Rochefoucauld, and Racine, may be seen as something like the definitive expression of a new paradigm—to be followed by refiners, exploiters, and popularizers of calculus, like Guillaume de l'Hospital—himself a contemporary of such eighteenth-century postclassicizing writers as La Grange-Chancel, Longepierre, or Houdart de la Motte.

In another context meanwhile, comparison of several versions of the Phaedra legend reveals consistent time-specific changes in their Greimasian actantial distribution and narrative function. At the same time comparison of Jean Auvray's *L'Innocence descouverte* of 1609 or 1628 with Racine's masterpiece *Phèdre* of 1677 reveals a striking time-specific difference in the nature of the metaphorical unity that structures the two texts, from relatively more organic to relatively more schematized and intellectualized structure, the latter expressed through a narrative key. Comparison of La Fontaine's *Astrologue qui se laisse tomber dans un puits* of 1668 with his *Un Animal dans la lune* of 1677 suggests movement toward a world in which, henceforth, "la raison décide en maîtresse." Such a comparison also suggests movement away from metaphorical unity as a universal structuring principle toward unity based on consistency of a relatively more philosophical sort. From a narrative standpoint the same movement does serious damage to the patterns of traditional narrative structures, which make La Fontaine's earlier fables and tales susceptible to analyses like those of Propp's folktales or Lévi-Strauss's myths—later fables lending themselves best to narrative analysis of a more *savante* or more intellectual kind.

Each of these analyses gains its rigor from concentration on two specific texts exhibiting striking resemblances and striking differences. Clearly, however, each of the suggestions could be extended to a considerable variety of texts from the corresponding periods. Thus differences between Du Bellay's Anet and Ronsard's Saint-Cosme surely relate to a very wide body of late sixteenth- and early seventeenth-century poetry recently analyzed in a Foucaldian vein by a variety of specialists, investigating D'Aubigné, Bertaut, Malherbe, Théophile, Tristan, and Saint-Amant, among others. Montaigne's and Charron's views of thinking and critique of the product of thought could be extended to Honoré d'Urfé's moralizing works, to Desportes, to

Malherbe, to Régnier, and Saint François de Sales, among others. Meanwhile, the mathematicizing of human endeavor may be observed not only in Thibault's *Académie* but also in treatises on medicine, gardening, painting, natural history, and sexual intercourse—not to mention such manuals of thought itself as Arnauld and Nicole's *Logique de Port-Royal.* In the same way the "post-crisis baroque" synthesis of the later *Tyr et Sidon* has its analogues in much of the so-called later baroque theater—Mairet, Corneille's *Le Menteur,* and the works of Rotrou, for example. The repertoire of "practical reason," moreover, goes well beyond the works of Corneille to include the apparently bourgeois, moderating morality of Molière, the *amour-propre* of La Rochefoucauld, or the play of *esprit de géométrie* and *esprit de finesse* in Pascal. The movement of practical reason between Garnier's *Bradamante* and Corneille's *Le Cid* finds other analogues, moreover, in the Phaedra plays of Garnier, Yeuwain, La Pinelière, and Gilbert. Movement of metaphorical unity and movement toward the preeminence of reason, finally, are carried further in Racine's Saint-Cyr plays, in the later fabulists, and the like.

In one context or another, therefore, this book mentions most major authors of the late sixteenth century and the whole of the seventeenth. And the analyses presented in detail, while far from being a complete, rigorous description—or even one exclusive of counterexamples on specific points—nevertheless may have significant general application. Indeed, when taken as wholes, the specific examples and conclusions may well be characteristic of the movement of French intellect between 1557 and 1719 and beyond.

Some of the interpretations to which they point are suggestive, certainly. At the level of intellectual history, the examples studied here may remind the historian of the real role of chronology in literary investigations. For in chronological reality, Malherbe is not the author of a single supposedly baroque poem, later repudiated, but a poet whose epistemological evolution parallels the supposedly baroque Desportes's and whose reforms represent only a small part of the poet's later career. In the same way the baroque poet Saint-Amant, at first the contemporary and the adversary of Malherbian reforms, becomes in later life an apologist of a relatively rationalistic or classicist approach to poetry, one very similar to that of the younger—almost contemporary —La Fontaine. In the same way—an extensively studied example—

Corneille evolves from a period in which he boasts that he will not always observe the emerging rules of French classicism to a period in which he examined those rules at length and modified his works extensively to conform to them. Having begun his poetic career in the later decades of a supposedly baroque epoch, Corneille lived to write plays with a very different, even Racinian worldview. Both Racine and La Fontaine, having gained celebrity in the so-called classical moment of 1660–80, lived to become the contemporaries of writers more often studied by specialists of the eighteenth century than the seventeenth — not only Longepierre and similar dramatists, but Bayle, Fontenelle, and Voltaire. In general, a literary historian might appropriately deduce from these examples that the academic custom of making specialties of one or another of the "centuries" of French literature has obscured the movement of intellectual preoccupations between 1580 and 1620, as well as between 1680 and 1720 or any other similar chronological division.

At another level the examples given here may contribute something to the understanding of concepts commonly used to describe time-specific aspects of intellect. Taken together, these examples suggest that epistemological considerations may be a common ground, a unifying plane, or, as Pascal writes, the "sens auquel tous les passages contraires s'accordent" ["sense in which all the contrary passages come together"] in such apparently disparate but apparently coexisting phenomena as mannerist malaise or baroque playfulness, precious refinement or grotesque horror, classicist economy and burlesque extravagance — or indeed any of the five or eight or otherwise-numbered categories of baroque and accompanying literary styles. Any intellectual situation, of course, admits of diverse responses — even creates and defines a repertoire of possible responses. It is in this sense that intuitively perceived "period styles" like the much-debated baroque — or such time-specific techniques as Hubert's metaphorical unity — may welcome rather than reject, reduce, or gloss over the very real intellectual diversity of the period. Any epistemological issue, after all, may be brooded about or laughed at; any new paradigm of language may be worked out through attempts to purify language or through attempts to caricature its suddenly deconsecrated possibilities; any mathematizing, regularizing procedure may seek classical Dampfung or burlesque caricature.[1]

In such a context the various phenomena attributed to mannerism, to the baroque style, the metaphysical disquietude of Sponde or Yeuwain, or the epistemological play of Saint-Amant or Schélandre may plausibly be interpreted as events taking place within an "epistemological space" —an *épistémè* of resemblance somehow transformed into an *épistémè* of representation.

The "somehow" of the matter suggests that *Les Mots et les choses*' description gains much from various sorts of empirical tinkering, in particular from Kuhn's description of so-called scientific revolutions. Described by Foucault himself as "admirable and definitive," Kuhn's account has the advantage of transforming perhaps mysterious "archeological" change into mechanisms based on the more or less conscious decisions of individuals pursuing more or less definable, practical ends. As such it attempts to link two possibly irreconcilable substances— Foucaldian archeology and the movement of thought.[2]

For such a purpose Kuhn's account of intellectual change is itself subject to tinkering, of course. As the preceding pages have occasionally suggested, Ronsard may not always have behaved like Galileo, and Honoré d'Urfé or Thibault may not always have experienced crisis or assimilated novelty in the same way as Descartes or Newton or Lavoisier. Seventeenth-century libertines or classicists, responding to imperatives only partially corresponding to Kuhn's, may not always have behaved like members of the contemporary American scientific community.

In part because of the limitations of the comparative method I have adopted, this work stops short of describing all those intermediate decisions which may fall, so to speak, between the examples presented. Similarly, it has had very little to say about all those social, economic, or other events, or, as they say, "forces," which may have motivated decisions to put words on paper. Nevertheless it suggests that a great deal of what appears here can be well understood as intellectual movement something like that described by Foucault and actually worked out through mechanisms something like those described by Kuhn: from resemblance, to crisis, to casting about and coexistence, to assimilation, to representation, so to speak.[3]

Whatever the purely "historical" account may be, partially Kuhnian, partially post-Kuhnian or para-Kuhnian, or the like, the examples presented here profit most, perhaps, from Kuhn's suggestion that one key to intellectual change is the willingness to use old tools in a new manner. Kuhn writes: "Since new paradigms are born from old ones, they ordinarily incorporate much of the vocabulary and apparatus, both conceptual and manipulative, that the traditional paradigm had previously employed. But they seldom employ these borrowed elements in quite the traditional way. Within the new paradigm, old terms, concepts, and experiments fall into new relationships one with the other." Just as a rococo architect may use the same basic decorative motifs as his neoclassicist or baroque predecessor—producing nevertheless a work in the rococo style—so Ronsard uses motifs similar to some in Du Bellay; Corneille uses motifs similar to some in Garnier; Racine uses some of the same metaphors as Auvray; and La Fontaine some of the commonplaces of earlier poetry—to produce works whose differences are nevertheless unmistakable. From a Kuhnian point of view the principles governing such transformations take on a special importance in times of changing styles. Kuhn writes: "When scientists disagree about whether the fundamental problems of their field have been solved, the search for rules gains a function that it does not ordinarily possess," a thought which might profitably be applied to the well-documented doctrinal controversies of the emerging decades of French classicism.[3]

In this Foucaldian/Kuhnian context, the literature and intellectual advances of the French seventeenth century—traditionally celebrated as the product of a *Grand Siècle*—may also take their place in a somewhat different intellectual construct. Described by Henri Peyre as an "accord momentané entre la faculté de penser et la faculté de sentir" ["a momentary coincidence of the faculty of thought and the faculty of feeling"] and described by others as a phenomenon of freedom and richness or bipolarity and opposites, the *Grand Siècle* and its celebrated classical moment may profitably be described also as a product of intellectual transition: not transition in the same way that anything at all may somehow be the transition between what precedes it and what follows—but instead, in the context suggested above, classicism appears as one possible means of assimilation of a new paradigm, and the masterpieces of French classicism as so many artifacts of assimilation, sharing their epoch with precious, burlesque, later mannerist, and later baroque artifacts as well.[4]

It might thus be concluded from the preceding pages that, as some others have recently suggested, French classicism also represents—as much as it may be a summit of French literature—a moment of aberration, the beginnings of a passing anomaly of Western civilization. As such it would stand at the beginning of a period in which, as Gérard Genette writes:

Pendant deux siècles (le XVIIe et le XVIIIe), et surtout en France, cette tendance "naturelle" à la valorisation (et parfois à la surestimation) du rapport analogique a été refoulée—ce qui n'était sans doute pas la bonne façon de la "psychanalyser"—par l'objectivisme répressif propre à l'éthos classique, qui considérait à priori toute métaphore comme suspecte d'excès fantasmatique, et tenait soigneusement en lisière l'imagination "symbolique." On sait comment le romantisme et le symbolisme lui ont rendu la liberté . . .

[For two centuries (the seventeenth and eighteenth), and especially in France, this "natural" tendency to value (and sometimes to overvalue) the analogical relation was repressed—which was no doubt not the best way to "psychoanalyze" it—by the classicist ethos's repressive objectivism, which considered any metaphor to be suspect, a priori, of fantastic excess and which carefully kept at arm's length the "symbolic" imagination. We know now how romanticism and symbolism liberated it . . .].

Thus the true place of classicism in the history of intellectual movement may be that of the beginning of an age of artificiality and repression—in the terms of the preceding pages of an artificial normalizing of the object of literature. It is for this reason perhaps that the classical writer, as André Gide writes somewhere, "s'efforce vers la banalité" ["strives for banality"]. In this light the classical writers and the classical master-pieces may have interest of a special, reverse or perverse sort for any age which, like our own, may be emerging from—or reentering—a period of artificiality and repression. As such classicism may be less the literature of the discovery of man in his universality, as traditional literary history suggests, than a discovery of an artificial image of the self.[5]

However this may be, the preceding pages suggest additionally that changes occurring between 1557 and 1719 also represent a profound transformation in the nature and function of literature as perceived by contemporary writers and readers alike. Whereas in the sixteenth century, literature is the proper description and celebration of the world, only to become in the last decades of that century a vehicle for epistemological speculation, by the later decades of the seventeenth century literature has become something very different—the exploration of value and contingency in a world whose ultimate knowledge is beginning to be contained in other, more scientific, and hence presumably more exact disciplines—a world which "Aux miracles de l'art fait céder la nature."

Whereas in the sixteenth century the poet or the essayist may stand as close as any other *chercheur* to the world's ultimate truths, by the eighteenth century writers express verities whose ultimate verification comes from domains exterior to literature. Literature itself changes as a consequence: poetry declines—the Foucaldian view coincides here with a traditional one—and for a time the theater, as a kind of battleground or dialectical arena or exemplification of competing worldviews, dominates the literary imagination, before being replaced at the end of the seventeenth century by narrative or expository prose. The latter is the preferred vehicle of expression in the Age of Reason or—in Kuhnian terms—the "normal literature" of a new paradigm.

Finally, it may well appear from the examples presented and the conclusions that they surely do not prove but certainly suggest that the difficulties involved in describing intellectual movement—and in particular the methodologically unsatisfying empiricist tinkering suggested above—may be due finally to the notions of synchrony and diachrony themselves. That is, this prominent problem of recent intellectual history is itself—like so many of its kind—the creation of the conceptual structure in which it appears, a kind of built-in flaw in the optics of the present-day intellectual paradigm that creates it. Perhaps the most striking statement on the problems of synchrony and diachrony in all of recent criticism is that of A. J. Greimas in his analysis of a story by Maupassant:

> ...la description de l'histoire fondamentale, conçue comme une suite de transformations des structures profondes, n'exclut pas, bien au contraire, sa projection sur l'axe de la temporalité.... A ne prendre, pour illustrer cette constatation, qu'un détail de l'histoire de la langue française: si le passage du français ancien, langue à déclinaison, en français moderne, langue sans déclinaison, apparaît comme une transformation structurelle, ce changement s'étale, au niveau de la temporalité de surface, sur une période de quelque trois cents ans, où les transformations discursives partielles, les procédures de médiation et de suppléance ont eu tout le temps de se manifester.

> [... the description of fundamental history, conceived as a succession of transformations of the deep structures, does not exclude, quite the contrary, its projection on the axis of temporality.... To take just one detail of the history of the French language to illustrate this conclusion, if the passage from Old French, a declensional

language, to Modern French, a non-declensional language, appears as a structural transformation, that change is spread out, at the level of surface temporality, over a period of some three hundred years, in which the partial discursive transformations, the processes of mediation and replacement have had time to be manifested].[6]

Whatever the mechanism of discourse, mediation, and replacement, it is clearly some such kind of schema that is represented in the preceding pages.

Paradoxically, despite its particularist and empiricist base, the preceding description thus presents a view of intellectual evolution which is—in many respects at least, adequate to its object. There are two reasons for this. First, the preceding pages may hope, like any other presentation, to offer explanation of some phenomena not hitherto explained. In particular it can "explain" and subsume notions of period style as understood and widely disagreed about up to now, in terms of Foucaldian and Kuhnian descriptions of intellectual movement: mannerism and one sort of baroque style moving toward crisis and a second baroque style and classicism moving away from it, assimilating a new paradigm. Second, offering some advantages over the model implied by the concepts of synchrony and diachrony, it may be said to "show" movement in the same way that a stock market ticker shows movement—that is, as the aggregate of numerous diversely motivated or even contradictory movements. Some have argued that in the world, as in the financial markets, there is no actually existing, static synchrony. By the same token, of course, there is no actually existing diachrony either. What there is, is the ·corpus of texts, the set of all affirmations. Each one—and particularly so in the case of books, which are composed of pages written and performed or published or translated on a given particular day—is a discrete textual artifact. The reality of diachrony is not the infinity of points of the geometrical line, not the curve of analytic geometry or calculus, but a series of discrete points whose interconnections are a matter for conjecture—so many discrete, but only partially accidental products of French seventeenth-century thought.

NOTES

1. Pascal, *Pensées,* p. 246.
2. Foucault, "Foucault Responds/2," 60.
3. Kuhn, *Structure of Scientific Revolutions,* pp. 48, 149.
4. Peyre, *Qu'est-ce que le classicisme,* p. 262.
5. Genette, *Figures III* (Paris: Seuil, 1972), p. 39.
6. Greimas, *Maupassant* (Paris: Seuil, 1976), pp. 26–27.

BIBLIOGRAPHY OF WORKS CITED

WORKS WRITTEN BEFORE 1800

Adam, Antoine, ed. *Romanciers du XVIIᵉ siècle*. Paris: Pléiade, 1958.

L'Adamite ou le jésuite insensible. Cologne, 1684.

Allem, M., ed. *Anthologie de la poésie française. XVIIᵉ siècle*. Paris: Garnier-Flammarion, 1966.

Aretino, Pietro. *Les Ragionamenti*. Anon. Fr. translation. Paris: Cercle Europeen du Livre, 1971.

Auvray, Jean. *Banquet des muses*. Rouen: J. Petit, 1628.

———. *Marfilie*. Rouen, 1609. Rpt. as *L'Innocence descouverte*, 1628.

Bidar, Mathieu. *Hippolyte*. Lille, 1675.

Bosse, Abraham. *Le Peintre converty aux précises et universelles règles de son art*. Edited by R.-A. Weigert. Paris: Hermann, 1964.

Bourdin, le Père. *Cours de mathématiques*. Paris, 1661.

Charron, Pierre. *De la sagesse*. Paris, 1604.

———. *De la sagesse*. Paris, 1607.

———. *De la sagesse*. Paris, 1789.

Corneille, Pierre. *Théâtre complet*. 3 vols. Paris: Garnier, n.d.

Descartes, René. *Géométrie*. Translated by D. E. Smith and M. L. Latham. La Salle, Ill.: Open Court, 1952.

———. *Oeuvres et lettres*. Edited by A. Bridoux. Paris: Pléiade, 1953.

Desportes, Philippe. *Les Amours de Diane*. Vol. 1. Edited by Victor E. Graham. Geneva: Droz, 1959.

———. *Les Amours d'Hippolyte*. Edited by Victor E. Graham. Geneva: Droz, 1960.

———. *Diverses amours et autres oeuvres meslées*. Edited by Victor E. Graham. Geneva: Droz, 1963.

Garnier, Robert. *Bradamante*. Edited by M. Hervier. Paris: Garnier, 1949.

———. *Oeuvres complètes*. Vol. 2. Edited by L. Pinvert. Paris: Garnier, 1923.

Gilbert, Gabriel. *Hypolite ou le garçon insensible*. Paris, 1647.

Gomberville, Marin le Roy de. *Polexandre*. 5 vols. Paris, 1637–42.

Goujet, Abbé. *Bibliothèque française*. 18 vols. Paris, 1740–56.

Houdart de la Motte, Antoine. *L'Esprit des poésies*. Geneva, 1767.

La Fontaine, Jean de. *Oeuvres complètes*. Edited by J. Marmier. Paris: Seuil, 1965.

———. *Oeuvres diverses*. Edited by P. Clarac. Paris: Pléiade, 1948.

La Marinière. *La Maison académique*. Paris, 1654.

La Pinelière, Guérin de. *Hippolyte, tragédie.* Paris, 1635.

L'Hospital, Guillaume de. *Analyse des infiniment petits.* Paris, 1696.

Longepierre, Hilaire-Bernard de Requeleyne, baron de. *Médée.* Edited by T. Tobari. Paris: Nizet, 1967.

Malherbe, François de. *Oeuvres poétiques.* Edited by R. Fromilhague and R. Lebègue. 2 vols. Paris: Les Belles Lettres, 1968.

Millot [or Mililot], Michel. *Escole des filles.* Paris: Eurodif, 1979.

Montaigne, Michel de. *Essais.* Edited by A. Thibaudet. Paris: Pléiade, 1950.

Mort aux pipeurs. Paris, 1608.

Pascal, Blaise. *Oeuvres complètes.* Edited by L. Lafuma. Paris: Seuil, 1963.

―――. *Pensées.* Edited by L. Lafuma. Paris: Delmas, 1960.

Racine, Jean. *Théâtre complet.* Edited by M. Rat. Paris: Garnier, 1960.

Ramus, Pierre de la Ramée dit. *Gramère (1562): Grammaire (1572); Dialectique (1555).* Rpt. Geneva: Slatkine, 1972.

Ronsard, Pierre de. *Oeuvres complètes.* Vol. 17. Edited by P. Laumonnier, I. Silver, and R. Lebègue. Paris: Didier, 1959.

Saint-Amant, Antoine Girard de. *Oeuvres.* Edited by J. Bailbé and J. Lagny. 4 vols. Paris: Didier, 1969–71.

Saint-Didier, Henri de. *Traicté...sur l'espee seule....* Paris, 1573. Rpt. Paris: Soc. du Livre d'Art Ancien et Moderne, 1907.

Schélandre, Jean de. *Tyr et Sidon.* Edited by J. W. Barker. Paris: Nizet, 1974.

Schérer, Jacques, ed. *Théâtre du XVIIᵉ siècle.* Paris: Pléiade, 1975.

Schmidt, A.-M., ed. *Poètes du XVIᵉ siècle.* Paris: Pléiade, 1953.

Sorel, Charles. *La Maison des jeux.* 2 vols. Paris, 1642.

Thibault, Girard. *Académie de l'espée.* Brussels, 1628.

Urfé, Honoré d'. *L'Astrée.* Edited by H. Vaganay. 5 vols. Lyon: Masson, 1928.

―――. *Les Tres Veritables Maximes,* extraits de l'*Astrée* by H. Vaganay. Lyon: H. Lardanchet, 1913.

Viète, François. *Opera Mathematica.* Hildesheim: G. Olms, 1970.

Yeuwain, Jean. *Hippolyte.* Edited by G. Van Severen. Mons: L. Pequeone, 1933.

WORKS WRITTEN AFTER 1900

Adam, Antoine. *Histoire de la littérature française au XVIIᵉ siècle.* 5 vols. Paris: Domat, 1948–62.

Ariès, Philippe, and André Béjin, eds. "Sexualités occidentales," a special issue of *Communications* 35 (1982).

Baïche, André. *La Naissance du baroque.* Lille: Sv. reprod. thèses, 1973.

Barthes, Roland. *Sade, Fourier, Loyola.* Paris: Seuil, 1971.

Baudrillard, Jean. *Oublier Foucault.* Paris: Galilée, 1977.

Belaval, Yvon. *Leibnitz critique de Descartes.* Paris: Gallimard, 1960.

Blanche, Robert. *La Logique et son histoire.* Paris: A. Colin, 1970.

Bloomberg, Edward. "Etude sémantique du mot 'raison' chez Pascal." *OL* 28 (1973): 124–37.

Borgerhoff, E. B. O. *The Freedom of French Classicism.* Princeton: University of Princeton Press, 1950.

Boyer, Carl B. *History of the Calculus and Its Conceptual Development.* New York: Dover, 1949.

Brody, Jules, ed. *French Classicism: A Critical Miscellany.* Englewood Cliffs, N.J.: Prentice-Hall, 1966.

Buffum, Imbrie. *Studies in the Baroque from Montaigne to Rotrou.* New Haven: Yale University Press, 1957.

Chomsky, Noam. *Cartesian Linguistics.* New York: Harper, 1966.

Courtès, Joseph. *Introduction à la sémiotique narrative et discursive. Méthodologie et application.* Paris: Hachette, 1976.

Croce, Benedetto. *Esthetics.* Translated by D. Ainslie. New York: Noonday, 1953.

Dabney, Lancaster E. *French Dramatic Literature in the Reign of Henri IV.* Austin: University Cooperative Society, 1952.

Davidson, Hugh M. "Yet Another View of French Classicism." *Bucknell Review* 13 (1965): 51–62.

Deleuze, Gilles. *Différence et Répétition.* Paris: P.U.F., 1968.

————. *Un Nouvel Archiviste.* Montpellier: Fata Morgana, 1972.

Dormon, Pierre. *Le Mythe de la procréation à l'âge baroque.* Paris: Pauvert, 1977.

Dubois, C.-G. *Le Baroque.* Paris: Larousse, 1973.

Ehrmann, Jacques, ed. "The Classical Line," a special issue of *Yale French Studies* 38 (1967).

Feyerabend, Paul. *Against Method.* London: Verso, 1978.

Foucault, Michel. "Foucault Responds/2." *Diacritics* 1 (1971): 60.

————. *Histoire de la folie. Folie et déraison à l'âge classique.* Paris: Plon, 1961.

————. *Les Mots et les choses.* Paris: Gallimard, 1966.

————. *La Volonté de savoir. Histoire de la sexualité.* Paris: Gallimard, 1976.

Francis, Claude. *Les Métamorphoses de "Phèdre" dans la littérature française.* Quebec: Pélican, 1967.

François, Carlo. *La Notion de l'absurde dans la littérature française du XVIIe siècle.* Paris: Klincksieck, 1973.

Galan, F. W. "Literary System and Systemic Change: The Prague School Theory of Literary History, 1928–48." *PMLA* 94 (1979): 275–85.

Genette, Gérard. *Figures III.* Paris: Seuil, 1972.

George, Richard T., and Fernande M., de. *The Structuralists: From Marx to Lévi-Strauss.* New York: Anchor, 1972.

Girard, René. *La Violence et le sacré*. Paris: Grasset, 1974.

Goux, Jean-Joseph. "La Logique des classiques." *TelQ* no. 24 (1965): 85–91.

Greimas, A.-J. "The Cognitive Dimension of Narrative Discourse." *NLH* (1976): 433–47.

———. *Du Sens*. Paris: Seuil, 1970.

———. *Maupassant*. Paris: Seuil, 1976.

Gutting, Gary, ed. *Paradigms and Revolutions*. South Bend, Ind.: Notre Dame University Press, 1980.

Haight, Jeanne. *The Concept of Reason in French Classical Literature*. Toronto: University of Toronto Press, 1982.

Hallyn, Fernand. *Formes métaphoriques dans la poésie lyrique de l'âge baroque en France*. Geneva: Droz, 1975.

Harth, Erica. "Exorcising the Beast: Attempts at Rationality in French Classicism." *PMLA* 88(1973): 19–24.

Hauser, Arnold. *Mannerism*. London: Routledge, 1965.

Hubert, J. D. *Essai d'exégèse racinienne*. Paris: Nizet, 1956.

———. "Malherbe à l'assaut du Parnasse." *ECr* 16 (1976): 105–15.

———. *Molière and the Comedy of Intellect*. Berkeley and Los Angeles: University of California Press, 1962.

Kay, W. B. *The Theatre of Jean Mairet: The Metamorphosis of Sensuality*. The Hague: Mouton, 1975.

Kogel, Renée. *Pierre Charron*. Geneva: Droz, 1972.

Köhler, E. "Je ne sais quoi; ein Kapitel aus der Begriffsgeschichte des Unbefreiflichen." *RJa* 6 (1953–54): 21–59.

Kuhn, Thomas S. *The Structure of Scientific Revolutions*. Chicago: University of Chicago Press, 1962 and 1970.

Lagny, Jean. *Le Poète Saint-Amant*. Paris: Nizet, 1964.

Lancaster, Henry Carrington. "Alexandre Hardy et ses rivaux." *RHL* 24 (1917): 414–21.

———. *History of French Dramatic Literature in the Seventeenth Century*. Vol. 1. Baltimore: Johns Hopkins University Press, 1929.

Ley, Herbert De. " 'Dans les reigles du plaisir': Transformations of Sexual Knowledge in Seventeenth-Century France." *Onze nouvelles études . . . de la femme*, ed. W. Leiner (Tübingen: G. Narr, 1984). Rpt., in different form, *Eroticism: French Literature Conference*. Columbia: University of South Carolina Press, 1983.

———. "Deux érotismes, deux modes de pensée dans les *Galanteries du duc d'Ossonne*." In *La Cohérence intérieure*, edited by J. Van Baelen and David Lee Rubin. Paris: J.-M. Place, 1977.

Lovejoy, A. O. *The Great Chain of Being*. Cambridge: Harvard University Press, 1936.

Macklem, Michael. *The Anatomy of the World: Relations between Natural and Moral Law from Donne to Pope*. Minneapolis: University of Minnesota Press, 1958.

Marin, Louis. *La Critique du discours*. Paris: Minuit, 1975.

Martin, Henri-Jean. *Livre, Pouvoirs et société à Paris au XVIIe siècle*. 2 vols. Geneva: Droz, 1969.

Martindale, Colin. *The Romantic Progression*. Washington, D.C.: Hemisphere, 1975.

Mehlman, Jeffrey. *A Structural Study of Autobiography*. Ithaca: Cornell University Press, 1974.

Michéa, R. "Les variations de la raison au XVIIe siècle." *Rev. Philos. de la France et de l'Etranger* 126 (1938): 183–201. Rpt. J. Brody, ed. *French Classicism*. New York: Prentice-Hall, 1966.

Moore, W. G. *French Classical Literature: An Essay*. London: Oxford, 1961.

Mornet, Daniel. *Histoire de la littérature française classique (1660–1700)*. . . . 3d ed. Paris: A. Colin, 1947.

Mourgues, Odette de. *O muse, fuyante proie*. . . . Paris: Corti, 1962.

Nelson, Robert J. "The Bipolarity of French Classicism." *EFL* no. 8 (1971): 11–28.

_____. "Modern Criticism of French Classicism." *Bucknell Review* 13 (1965): 37–50.

Paris, Jean. *Rabelais au futur*. Paris: Seuil, 1970.

Pedersen, John. *Images et figures dans la poésie française de l'âge baroque*. Etudes romanes de l'Université de Copenhagen, *Revue Romane* n° spéciale 5 (1974).

Peyre, Henri. "Common-Sense Remarks on the French Baroque." In *Studies . . . Morris Bishop*, edited by J. J. Demorest. Ithaca: Cornell University Press, 1962.

_____. *Qu'est-ce que le classicisme*. New ed. Paris: Nizet, 1965.

Piaget, Jean. *La Causalité physique chez l'enfant*. Paris: F. Alcan, 1927.

_____. *Structuralism*. London: Routledge, 1971.

Piel, Jean, ed. "Michel Serres: interférences et turbulences," *Critique* 380 (1979).

Ponge, Francis. *Pour un Malherbe*. Paris: Gallimard, 1965.

Racevskis, Karlis. *Michel Foucault and the Subversion of Intellect*. Ithaca: Cornell University Press, 1983.

Raymond, Marcel, and A. J. Steele, eds. *La Poésie française et le maniérisme. 1546–1610 (?)*. Geneva: Droz, 1971.

Reiss, T. J. *The Discourse of Modernism*. Ithaca: Cornell University Press, 1982.

_____, ed. "Science, Language, and the Perceptive Mind. Studies in Literature and Thought from Campanella to Bayle," *Yale French Studies* no. 49 (1973).

Ridgely, Beverly S. "Astrology and Astronomy in the *Fables* of La Fontaine." *PMLA* 80 (1965): 180–89.

Romanowski, Sylvie. *L'Illusion chez Descartes. La Structure du discours cartésien*. Paris: Klincksieck, 1974.

Rousset, Jean. *L'Intérieur et l'extérieur*. Paris: Corti, 1968.

————. *La Littérature de l'âge baroque en France. Circé et le paon.* Paris: Corti, 1954.

Rubin, David Lee. *Higher Hidden Order: Design and Meaning in the Odes of Malherbe.* Chapel Hill: University of North Carolina Press, 1972.

Serres, Michel. *Hermes I.* Paris: Seuil, 1968.

————. "Le Jeu du loup." In *Savoir, faire, espérer.* Brussels: Fac. St. Louis, 1976.

————. *Le Système de Leibnitz et ses modèles mathématiques.* Paris: P.U.F., 1968.

Shearman, John. *Mannerism.* Harmondsworth: Penguin, 1967.

Spitzer, Leo. "Die Kunst des Ubergangs bei La Fontaine." *PMLA* 53 (1938): 393–433.

Stone, Donald, Jr. "The Place of Garnier's *Bradamante* in Dramatic History." *AUMLA* 26 (1966): 260–71.

Sutcliffe, F. E. *Guez de Balzac et son temps; littérature et politique.* Paris: Nizet, 1959.

Tillyard, E. M. W. *The Elizabethan World Picture.* New York: Macmillan, 1944.

Truesdell, Clifford. "Reactions of Late Baroque Mechanics to Success, Conjecture, Error, and Failure in Newton's *Principia*." *Texas Quarterly* 10 (1967): 238–58.

Van Baelen, J., and David L. Rubin, eds. *La Cohérence intérieure. Etudes... Judd D. Hubert.* Paris: J.-M. Place, 1977.

Walker, Evelyn. *A Study of the "Traité des indivisibles" of Gilles Persone de Roberval....* New York: Teachers College, 1932.

Wellek, René. *Concepts of Criticism.* New Haven: Yale University Press, 1963.

Wölfflin, Heinrich. *Principles of Art History.* New York: Dover, n.d.

Zumthor, P., and H. Sommer. "A propos du mot 'génie.'" *ZRP* 66 (1950): 170–201.

Note on the Author

Herbert De Ley is professor of French at the University of Illinois at Urbana-Champaign. His previous publications include *Marcel Proust et le duc de Saint-Simon,* " '*Un Enchaînement si singulier . . .*'": *Saint-Simon Memorialist, Essay,* and articles in such journals as the *Yale French Studies, ECr, FR, and MLN.*